Introduction to RISC Assembly Language Programming

D0076816

Introduction to RISC Assembly Language Programming

JOHN WALDRON

School of Computer Applications
Dublin City University

 **Addison-Wesley**

Harlow, England • Reading, Massachusetts • Menlo Park, California
New York • Don Mills, Ontario • Amsterdam • Bonn • Sydney • Singapore
Tokyo • Madrid • San Juan • Milan • Mexico City • Seoul • Taipei

Pearson Education Limited
Edinburgh Gate
Harlow
Essex CM20 2JE
England

and Associated Companies throughout the World.

Visit us on the World Wide Web at:
http://www.pearsoneduc.com

© Addison Wesley Longman Limited 1999

The right of John Waldron to be identified as author of this Work has been asserted
by him in accordance with the Copyright, Designs and Patents Act 1988.

All rights reserved. No part of this publication may be reproduced, stored in a retrieval
system, or transmitted in any form or by any means, electronic, mechanical,
photocopying, recording or otherwise, without either the prior written permission of the
publisher or a licence permitting restricted copying in the United Kingdom issued by
the Copyright Licensing Agency Ltd, 90 Tottenham Court Road, London W1P 0LP.

The programs in this book have been included for their instructional value. They have
been tested with care but are not guaranteed for any particular purpose. The publisher
does not offer any warranties or representations nor does it accept any liabilities with
respect to the programs.

Many of the designations used by manufacturers and sellers to distinguish their
products are claimed as trademarks. Addison Wesley Longman Limited has made
every attempt to supply trademark information about manufacturers and their
products mentioned in this book. A list of the trademark designations and their
owners appears on page x.

Cover designed by OdB Design & Communication, Reading, UK
Typeset in 10/12pt Times by 32
Printed and bound in Great Britain by Henry Ling Ltd.,
at the Dorset Press, Dorchester, Dorset.

First printed 1998

ISBN 0-201-39828-1

British Library Cataloguing-in-Publication Data
A catalogue record for this book is available from the British Library

10 9 8 7 6 5 4
06 05 04 03 02

Preface

This book is based on a one-semester introductory computer architecture course for first-year computing students in the School of Computer Applications, Dublin City University, using SPIM, a virtual machine that runs programs for the MIPS R2000/R3000 computers. The architecture of the MIPS is an ideal example of a simple, clean RISC (Reduced Instruction Set Computer) machine, which makes it easy to learn and understand. The processor contains 32 general-purpose registers and a well-designed instruction set. The existence of a simulator for the processor greatly simplifies the development and debugging of assembly language programs. For these reasons, MIPS is the preferred choice for teaching computer architecture in the 2000s, just as the Motorola 68000 was during the 1980s.

The material assumes that the reader has never studied computer programming before, and is usually given at the same time as a programming course in a high-level language like Java or C. The main data structures covered are strings, arrays and stacks. The ideas of program loops, if statements, procedure calls and some recursion are presented. The philosophy behind the book is to speed up the learning process relative to other MIPS architecture books by enabling the reader to start writing simple assembly language programs early, without getting involved in laborious descriptions of the trade-offs involved in the design of the processor. The most successful approach to computer architecture is to begin by writing numerous small assembly language programs, before going on to study the underlying concepts. Thus this text does not address topics such as logic design or boolean algebra, but does contain example programs using the MIPS logical instructions. While processors like the MIPS were designed for high-level language compilation and as such are targeted at compilers rather than human programmers, the only way to gain an appreciation of their functionality is to write many programs for the processor in assembly language.

The book is associated with an automatic program testing system (Mips Assembly Language Exam System) which allows a lecturer to set assembly language programming questions and collect and mark the assignments automatically, or a reader to test a MIPS assembly language program against several different cases and determine whether it works, as described in Appendix A. The exam system is written as a collection of Unix C shell scripts. If the instructor or student does not wish to adopt this learning approach, the textbook can be used in a traditional manner. A student who can write an assembly language program which converts a number to an ASCII string in hexadecimal format under exam conditions has demonstrated a thorough understanding of all the principles of introductory computer architecture. There is little point in describing concepts such as pipelining, delayed branches of advanced compiler topics to students who are not yet familiar with simple program loops.

Assembly language programming is usually considered an arcane and complex discipline. This view arises among those whose first experience of assembly language programming was the instructions and registers of architectures like the Intel 8086 family. Programming in a RISC architecture is very different due to the elegant, compact and simple instruction set. Students of this text who have never programmed before and begin to study it simultaneously with a course on C programming report it is easier and more logical to program in assembly! In addition, because of the programming exam system, there is a higher pass rate and level of proficiency achieved by students on the assembly course than on the more traditional C course.

The SPIM simulator is available in the public domain from the University of Wisconsin Madison at `ftp://ftp.cs.wisc.edu/pub/spim/`. Overhead projector slides of lecture notes, all example programs and all exam questions are available from `http://www.compapp.dcu.ie/~jwaldron`. The programs that correct the questions, together with test cases and solutions, are available to lecturers adopting the course.

The SPIM simulator software was designed and written by James R. Laurus (laurus@cs.wisc.edu). This book was partly inspired by John Conry's course at the University of Oregon which he has made available on the Internet. I would like to thank him for permission to use some of his example programs and material. Thanks to Dr David Sinclair for reading an early draft and providing many important suggestions. Also thanks to Karen Sutherland and Keith Mansfield at Addison Wesley Longman.

John Waldron, Dublin
July 1998

Contents

Trademark Notice

Intel is a trademark of Intel Corporation.
Java is a trademark or registered trademark of Sun Microsystems, Inc.
Jurassic Park is a trademark or registered trademark of Amblin Entertainment.
Macintosh is a registered trademark of Apple Computer, Inc.
MIPS R2000 is a trademark or registered trademark of MIPS Technologies, Inc.
Motorola 68000 is a trademark or registered trademark of Motorola, Inc.
Nintendo 64 is a trademark or registered trademark of Nintendo of America, Inc.
SGI is a registered trademark of Silicon Graphics, Inc.
SPARC is a trademark of SPARC International Inc.
Star Wars is a trademark or registered trademark of Lucas Films.
Toy Story is a trademark, © Disney.
UNIX is a trademark, licensed through X/OPEN Company Ltd.

CHAPTER 1

Introduction

After describing basic computer organization, this chapter introduces assembly language, explains what it is and what it is used for. The reasons the reader should study assembly language are discussed. Finally, an outline of the remaining chapters in the book is given.

1.1 BASIC COMPUTER ORGANIZATION

The gates and flip-flops that collectively constitute the computer are built so that they can only assume one of two values or states called on and off. Each element of the computer can therefore represent only the values zero or one. Each one or zero is called a binary digit, or bit. The integrated circuits in a typical computer can be organized into three categories – the processor, the memory, and those connecting to various input output (I/O) devices such as disks or keyboards, as shown in Figure 1.1. The bus connects the integrated circuits together.

The processor is an integrated circuit that is the basic functional building block of the computer. It follows the fetch–execute cycle, repeatedly reading simple instructions, such as to add two numbers or move a number, from the memory and executing them as shown in Figure 1.2. The processor consists of:

- a data path, which performs arithmetic operations
- control, which tells the memory, I/O devices and data path what to do according to the wishes of the instructions of the program
- a small high-speed memory (registers) used to store temporary results and certain control information.

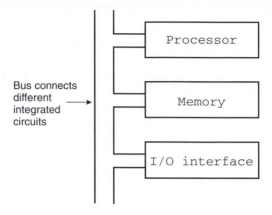

Figure 1.1 Integrated circuits in a computer.

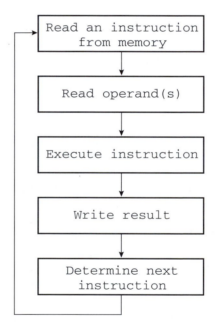

Figure 1.2 Fetch–execute cycle.

Electrically connected to the processor chip is the memory. Memory can be of various sizes, usually measured in multiples of megabytes or millions of bytes, where a byte is a group of eight bits. Also connected to the processor are I/O devices that allow the processor to communicate with the outside world through screens, keyboards and other information storage devices such as floppy disks or CD-ROMs.

All information in the memory and the processor registers must be represented by numbers. This includes the actual instructions themselves, as well as the information they operate on. The instructions of the processor manipulate numeric information in a variety of ways. Data can be moved from registers to memory or memory to registers. Data in registers is like data in memory, except that it can be accessed much faster. Data must be brought into registers for arithmetic operations such as addition, subtraction, multiplication and division, together with logical operations that allow manipulation of individual bits of information.

Some instructions do not manipulate data but are used to control the flow of a program, allowing an operation to be repeated several times for example.

1.2 MACHINE LANGUAGE

All instructions the processor executes are encoded as strings of bits and stored in the memory. If you write your programs directly in binary, using the encoding of instructions understood by the processor, you are writing in machine language. It's very tedious, and never done in practice.

1.3 ASSEMBLY LANGUAGE

A slightly more abstract version of machine language is assembly language. The term is a very old one – it goes back to the 1940s and 1950s when all programming was done in this sort of language. An assembler was a program that took symbols written by the programmer and assembled the final machine language program to be executed by the processor. There is usually a one-to-one correspondence between assembly language statements and machine language instructions. Instead of the binary pattern used in machine language, the assembly language programmer can write

```
add r0,r2,r3
```

to mean add the contents of registers two and three and put the result in register zero.

Assembly language provides other abstractions as well:

- labels on pieces of code; for example, if you write a subroutine (also known as a procedure) you can call it by name and use an instruction of the form `call printf` instead of something like 001010111100, which requires you to know the address of the procedure
- labels on variable names, with the same benefits as labels on code
- special assembly language instructions, called directives, that help you define data structures like strings and arrays.

An assembler can also hide many messy machine details from programmers. For example, the assembler can give the illusion that there are many more instructions in the processor than there really are, by providing pseudo-instructions which consist of several machine instructions, removing the one-to-one correspondence between assembly language and machine language instructions.

1.4 WHY PROGRAM IN ASSEMBLY LANGUAGE?

The most common reason to program in assembly language is that it is the best way to gain an understanding of how the processor and computer works at the lower levels. Apart from this it is generally better not to program in assembly language if you can do the same job in a high-level language like C and use a compiler to turn high-level language statements into sequences of machine instructions, as shown in Figure 1.3. Assembly language has the following disadvantages:

- Assembly language is not as tedious as machine language, but it is still error-prone and slow – the source code of programs is three or more times as long as corresponding programs in a high-level language such as C, and experience shows that people can write programs at a constant number of lines per day no matter what the language, so it will take three times as long to write the assembly language version. Also, the probability of introducing a bug is proportional to the length of the program.
- Assembly language is machine-dependent, so that a program written for a SPARC workstation (Sun) will have to be completely rewritten for DEC, SGI or IBM workstations. Assembly language programs are not portable.

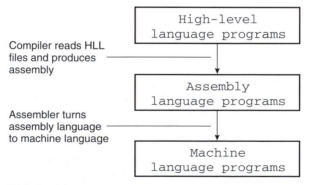

Figure 1.3 High-level languages.

- An assembly language program does not execute much faster than a high-level language program because compilers are getting to be very good, especially for machines with messy user-unfriendly features.

Sometimes assembly language is necessary:

- A special function inside the innermost loop of a critical program might be coded in assembly language.
- Assembly language may be best for embedded systems that have very little memory or a crucial timing problem where you need to know exactly how many machine cycles an operation will take.
- A few machine-specific operations in an operating system kernel must be coded in assembly.
- There are a large number of existing programs written in assembly language that need to be maintained and updated. A major UK airline's booking system is said to be written entirely in assembly language and that company places great value on those with assembly language programming skills.

When you do have to use assembly language, try to do it via a high-level language. Many C compilers will allow you to embed assembly language code in the middle of a C program, writing the body of a procedure in assembly language.

It is very important to learn assembly language programming because:

- When you program in a high-level language, it is essential to understand the underlying machine instructions when debugging your program.
- To write a compiler, it is necessary to be familiar with assembly language.
- People who design and build processors need to understand assembly language instruction sets.

In conclusion, the assembly language instruction set defines the interface between the hardware and the software and underlies all the functioning of a computer, so that a thorough appreciation of this topic is essential for any student of computer science or electronic engineering. It is this level of understanding that differentiates a computing graduate from say a maths or business student that has learnt to program.

1.5   OUTLINE OF CHAPTERS

Chapter 2 gives some essential background information needed before studying assembly language programming. Hexadecimal, decimal and binary numbers are explained. The way in which addition and subtraction are carried out on these numbers, together with the representation of negative numbers, is discussed. Also covered is the ASCII character code used to store characters in a computer's memory. An understanding of these concepts is essential before programming in any computer language, because all digital computers ultimately consist of large numbers of on/off switches.

Chapter 3 does not describe every detail of the MIPS processor, but gives enough information about memory and internal MIPS registers to allow simple assembly language programs to be written. The XSPIM simulator is introduced. A deeper understanding of the concepts introduced in this chapter will be developed as later chapters expand on them. It is necessary to have an idea of the architecture of the MIPS processor if one is to program it in assembly language.

Chapter 4 begins by outlining the syntax used in a MIPS assembly language program. It then considers a simple example program. The instructions used in this program are introduced. The XSPIM programming tool is then described. Detailed instructions for executing the example program using XSPIM are given. Additional simple load, store and arithmetic instructions are introduced, together with some example programs illustrating their use.

Chapter 5 looks at a program length.a that uses a program loop to work out the length of a character string. Familiarity with a few assembly language instructions, such as basic load, store and simple arithmetic operations, is needed, together with the concept of program loops. A program loop allows an operation to be repeated a number of times, without having to enter the assembly language instructions explicitly. For example, to sum up 50 numbers, one would not have 50 add instructions in the program but instead would have the add instruction once and go round a loop 50 times.

For any given operation, such as load, add or branch, there are often many different ways to specify the address of the operand(s). The different ways of determining the address are called addressing modes. Chapter 6 looks at the different addressing modes of the MIPS processor and shows how all instructions can fit into a single four-byte word. Some sample programs are included to show additional addressing modes in action.

Chapter 7 first looks at shift and rotate instructions. It then considers logical instructions, showing in an example program how these instructions can be used to convert a decimal number to an ASCII string in hexadecimal format. Logical, shift and rotate instructions are all used to manipulate the individual bits of a word.

Chapter 8 first introduces the stack data structure, and then illustrates its usage with a program to reverse a string using a stack. The techniques to support procedure calls in MIPS assembly language are then studied. Procedures allow programs to be broken into smaller, more manageable, units. They are fundamental to the development of programs longer than a few dozen statements. Procedures allow the reuse of the same group of statements many times by referring to them by name rather than repeating the code. In addition, procedures make large programs easier to read and understand. Stack frames, needed to implement procedure calls, are discussed. Two recursive programs are given that calculate Fibonacci's series and solve the Towers of Hanoi problem, and example code from a real compiler is discussed.

Appendix A describes the MIPS programming exam system. Appendix B is a SPIM MIPS instruction quick reference, sorted by instruction type. Appendix C is a more complete instruction reference in alphabetic order.

1.6   SUMMARY

Each element of the computer can represent only the values zero or one. The processor follows the fetch–execute cycle repeatedly reading simple instructions, such as to add two numbers or move a number, from the memory and executing them. All instructions that the processor executes are encoded as strings of bits, called machine language, and stored in the memory. An assembler is a program that takes symbols written by the programmer and assembles the final machine language program to be executed by the processor. The source code of assembly language programs is three or more times as long as corresponding high-level language programs. The assembly language instruction set defines the interface between the hardware and the software and underlies all the functioning of a computer so that a thorough appreciation of this topic is essential for any student of computer science or electronic engineering.

EXERCISES

1.1   What is register?
1.2   What does a processor do?
1.3   What do integrated circuits consist of?
1.4   Describe the principal integrated circuits in a computer.
1.5   Describe the relationship between machine language and assembly language.
1.6   What are the advantages of programming in assembly language over machine language?
1.7   When should assembly language be used?

CHAPTER 2

Essential background information

2.1   INTRODUCTION

This chapter gives some essential background information needed before studying assembly language programming. Hexadecimal, decimal and binary numbers are explained. The way in which addition and subtraction are carried out on these numbers, together with the representation of negative numbers, is discussed. Also covered is the ASCII character code used to store characters in a computer's memory. An understanding of these concepts is essential before programming in any computer language, because all digital computers ultimately consist of large numbers of on/off switches.

2.2   DECIMAL AND BINARY NUMBERS

Many different systems have been used to represent numbers throughout history. The Babylonians had a method of counting based on the number 60, and the effects of this can still be seen in measurements of time and angles. Our present system, of course, is based on the number of fingers on the human hand and is called the decimal number system, or base 10.

In the decimal number system, each digit's position represents a different power of 10. For example, the number 169 is equivalent to

$$1 \times 10^2 + 6 \times 10^1 + 9 \times 10^0$$

All digital computers use base 2, known as the binary system, for numerical quantities rather than base 10. Binary numbers are based on

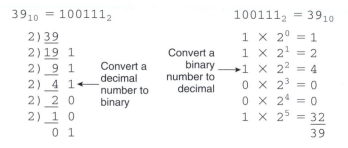

Figure 2.1 Conversion between binary and decimal numbers.

powers of 2 rather than on powers of 10. The number 1101 in the binary number system is equivalent to

$$1 \times 2^3 + 1 \times 2^2 + 0 \times 2^1 + 1 \times 2^0$$

The method of converting a binary number to decimal is straightforward and is shown in Figure 2.1. It involves adding up the powers of two everywhere the corresponding binary position contains a one.

Converting a decimal number to binary is not quite as simple. The way to do this is to divide the original decimal number by two and check the remainder. If the remainder is one, a binary one is generated. If it is zero, a binary zero is produced. This division by two is repeated until a zero quotient is obtained, as illustrated in Figure 2.1. This process yields the bits of the answer in reverse order.

Converting between decimal and binary is needed because humans think about numbers in decimal, but numbers will be stored as a sequence of bits in the computer.

2.3 HEXADECIMAL NUMBERS

Hexadecimal numbers, or hex for short, use base 16 to represent numerical quantities. Each hex digit can take on 16 values, which means that six extra symbols are needed on top of the 0 to 9 used for decimal. As shown in Figure 2.2 the letters A through F are used to represent the additional values 10 to 15. Lower-case a through f are also sometimes used with the same meaning. This book follows the convention of putting 0x before a number to indicate it is in hexadecimal format. The methods for converting between the hex and decimal number systems are also shown in Figure 2.2. The techniques for converting are the same as those illustrated in Figure 2.1 for the binary system.

The disadvantage of binary numbers is that once the number gets large, it becomes very tedious to write out a long string of ones and zeros. The advantage of binary is that it is possible to see by inspection how many bits

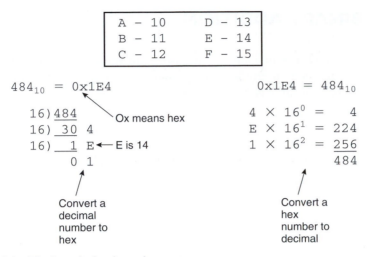

Figure 2.2   The hexadecimal number system.

are occupied by the number when stored in the computer, and which bits are set or cleared (i.e. one or zero). This would not be obvious if the number was in base 10. Even large hex numbers are short to write out, yet it is still possible to see by inspection how many bits are occupied by the number, and which bits are set or cleared. A nice property of hexadecimal numbers is that they can be converted to binary by inspection, as shown in Figure 2.3. Since

$$2^4 = 16$$

there is a simple relationship between numbers in base 2 and in base 16. Four binary digits grouped together represent one hexadecimal digit.

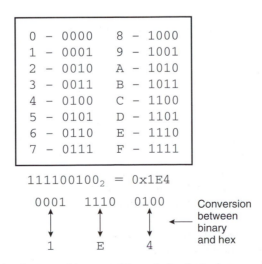

Figure 2.3   Conversion between binary and hexadecimal numbers.

2.4   BINARY ADDITION

The rules for addition of numbers in base 2 are simple, as shown in Figure 2.4. To add numbers in any base, if the sum of two digits equals or exceeds the number base, a carry is generated. The value of the carry is 1.

2.5   TWO'S COMPLEMENT NUMBERS

The discussion so far has only dealt with positive numbers. What about negative numbers and subtraction? Numeric quantities in a computer are normally restricted to fixed sizes, for example eight bits or 32 bits. It is not practical to append an extra sign bit, indicating plus or minus, to a fixed unit such as a byte. A better solution is to sacrifice one of the bits in a byte to indicate the sign of the number. The size of the largest number that can be represented is reduced, but both positive and negative numbers can now be represented.

All modern computers use the two's complement representation for negative numbers. The method of converting a decimal number to two's complement form is shown in Figure 2.5. If the number is positive, convert it to binary and fill out the most significant bits with zeros. If the number is negative, get the positive two's complement representation and multiply the number by -1. It is very easy to multiply a two's complement number by -1, thus changing its sign. The steps are (Figure 2.5):

- convert all the zero bits to one and all the one bits to zero
- add one to this number.

The sign bit or leftmost bit is used to indicate whether a number is positive or negative. By convention, if a numerical quantity is negative, the sign bit of the number is one. In two's complement form, if the number is negative and begins with a leading one, the remaining bits do not directly indicate the magnitude. Positive numbers begin with a zero and the other bits are the magnitude.

The two's complement method of representing numbers can be visualized as being arranged in a wheel as shown in Figure 2.6. Going clockwise increases a number, which means that adding numbers to a negative number causes the result to move in the direction of zero. The reason two's complement has been universally adopted is that the addition rules in Figure 2.4 can be used without concern for the sign of either number and still give the correct result. When the computer wishes to do subtraction involving two's complement numbers, it changes the sign of the subtrahend using the steps above and does an ordinary addition, as illustrated in Figure 2.7.

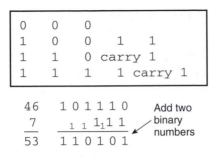

$$46 \quad 1\;0\;1\;1\;1\;0$$
$$\underline{7} \qquad \underline{1\;1\;1_1 1\;1}$$
$$53 \quad 1\;1\;0\;1\;0\;1$$

Add two
binary
numbers

Figure 2.4 Addition of numbers in base 2.

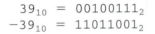

$$39_{10} = 00100111_2$$
$$-39_{10} = 11011001_2$$

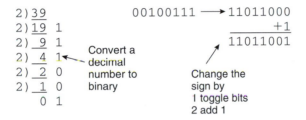

2)39
2)19 1
2) 9 1
2) 4 1
2) 2 0
2) 1 0
  0 1

Convert a
decimal
number to
binary

$00100111 \longrightarrow 11011000$
$$\underline{\qquad\qquad +1}$$
$$11011001$$

Change the
sign by
1 toggle bits
2 add 1

Figure 2.5 Eight-bit two's complement representation of numbers.

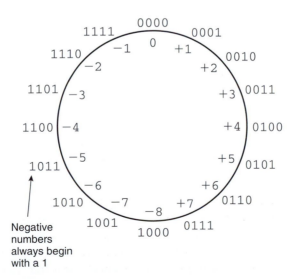

Negative
numbers
always begin
with a 1

Figure 2.6 Two's complement wheel.

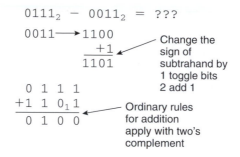

Figure 2.7 Subtraction of two's complement numbers.

2.6 BITS, BYTES AND NIBBLES

As mentioned above, the gates and flip-flops that collectively constitute the computer are built so that they can only assume one of two values or states. Bits in a computer are grouped together so that the internal representations of numbers are restricted to certain sizes. Nearly all computers are organized around groups of eight bits, called a byte or sometimes an octet. Four bytes grouped together are called a word. Confusingly on some older computers, two bytes are called a word. A nibble, four bits, is half a byte and can be described by one hex digit. There are 2^n different combinations of n bits. For example there are $2^8 = 256$ combinations that can be held in one byte. If the patterns are regarded as positive or unsigned numbers then the numbers run from 0 to $2^8 - 1 = 255$.

If the byte is holding signed numbers in two's complement format the numbers can range from -2^{n-1} to $+2^{n-1} - 1$. For example, in Figure 2.6, $n = 4$ and the 16 numbers range from -8 to $+7$.

2.7 STORING CHARACTERS

In order to represent character information in the computer's memory, the character set must be converted to numeric values. Two standard codes are used for this:

- ASCII: American Standard Code for Information Interchange
- EBCDIC: Extended Binary-Coded Decimal Interchange Code.

All microcomputers use the ASCII code (Figure 2.8) and EBCDIC is typically used by IBM mainframes.

Upper- and lower-case alphabetic characters, the digits 0 through 9 and the common punctuation marks are sufficient for many purposes – about a hundred characters in all. The ASCII code uses the values 0 to 127, corresponding to seven of the eight bits in a byte. The ASCII codes 0

Rightmost bits

Leftmost bits

	000	001	010	011	100	101	110	111
0000	NUL	DLE	SP	0	@	P	`	p
0001	SOH	DC1	!	1	A	Q	a	q
0010	STX	DC2	"	2	B	R	b	r
0011	ETX	DC3	#	3	C	S	c	s
0100	EOT	DC4	$	4	D	T	d	t
0101	ENQ	NAK	%	5	E	U	e	u
0110	ACK	SYN	&	6	F	V	f	v
0111	BEL	ETB	'	7	G	W	g	w
1000	BS	CAN	(	8	H	X	h	x
1001	HT	EM	)	9	I	Y	i	y
1010	LF	SUB	*	:	J	Z	j	z
1011	VT	EXC	+	;	K	[	k	{
1100	FF	FS	,	<	L	\	l		
1101	CR	GS	-	=	M	]	m	}
1110	SO	RS	.	>	N	^	n	~
1111	SI	US	/	?	O	-	o	DEL

ASCII 'a' = 1100001_2 = 0x61

ASCII '>' = 0111110_2 = 0x3E

Find the ASCII code of a character

Figure 2.8 ASCII character codes.

through 31 are reserved for special non-printing codes. These include CR (carriage return), LF (line feed) and HT (horizontal tab). Other ASCII codes in the range 0 through 31 are used for various purposes such as data communication protocols.

The Unicode Standard is a new international standard used to encode text for computer processing. Its design is based on the simplicity and consistency of ASCII, but goes far beyond ASCII's limited ability to encode only the Latin alphabet. The Unicode Standard provides the capacity to encode all of the characters used for the major written languages of the world. To accommodate the many thousands of characters used in international text, the Unicode Standard uses a 16-bit code set that provides codes for more than 65 000 characters. To keep character coding simple and efficient, the Unicode Standard assigns each character a unique 16-bit value. Mathematicians and technicians, who regularly use mathematical symbols and other technical characters, also find the Unicode Standard valuable.

2.8   SUMMARY

In the decimal number system, each digit's position represents a different power of 10, whereas binary numbers are based on powers of 2. The disadvantage of binary numbers is that once the number gets large, it becomes very tedious to write out a long string of ones and zeros. Hexadecimal, or hex for short, uses base 16 to represent numerical quantities because it is easy to switch between binary and hex. To add numbers in any base, if the sum of two digits equals or exceeds the number base, a carry is generated. The value of the carry is 1. All modern computers use the two's complement representation for negative numbers. In order to represent character information in the computer's memory, the characters can be converted to numeric values using the ASCII code.

EXERCISES

2.1   How is 300_{10} stored in binary?

2.2   Is bit six set or cleared when 300_{10} is stored in binary?

2.3   How many bits are required to store 300_{10} in binary?

2.4   What is 300_{10} in hex?

2.5   Write down the eight-bit two's complement binary representation of -78.

2.6   Write down the 32-bit two's complement representation of -32 in hexadecimal notation.

2.7   Show the steps involved when a computer subtracts 3 from 5.

2.8   What is the ASCII code for the semicolon?

CHAPTER 3

MIPS computer organization

3.1 INTRODUCTION

This chapter does not describe every detail of the MIPS processor, but gives enough information about memory and internal MIPS registers to allow simple assembly language programs to be written. The XSPIM simulator is introduced. A deeper understanding of the concepts introduced in this chapter will be developed as later chapters expand on them. It is necessary to have an idea of the architecture of the MIPS processor if one is to program it in assembly language.

3.2 THE MIPS DESIGN

In the mid-1970s, a number of studies showed that while theoretically people can write highly complex high-level language programs, most of the code that they actually write consists of simple assignments, `if` statements and procedure calls with a limited number of parameters (together 85 per cent). This is shown in Figure 3.1.

In the early 1980s, a new trend in the design of processors began with the RISC (Reduced Instruction Set Computer) machines. The central idea was that by speeding up the commonest simple instructions, one could afford to pay a penalty in the unusual case and make a large net gain in performance. In contrast CISC (Complex Instruction Set Computer) chips can execute many complicated instructions, at the expense of slowing down the simplest ones.

In 1980, a group at Berkeley, led by David Patterson and Carlo Sequin, began designing RISC chips. They coined the term RISC and named their

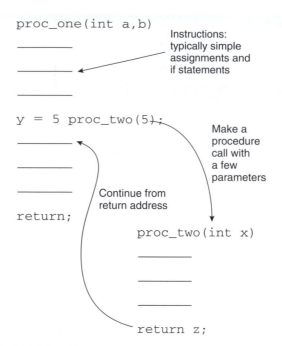

Figure 3.1 Typical high-level language program.

processor RISC1. Slightly later, in 1981, across the San Francisco Bay at Stanford, John Hennessy designed and fabricated a somewhat different RISC chip which he called the MIPS (Microprocessor without Interlocking Pipeline Stages), a play on the MIPS performance measurement.

MIPS processors are quite powerful, and are the heart of the capabilities of SGI's graphics servers and workstations, which were used to produce the special effects in many Hollywood movies (for example the new version of *Star Wars*, *Jurassic Park* and *Toy Story*). MIPS processors are also used in the Nintendo 64 game machine. Because of its use in high-performance embedded systems, it is estimated that MIPS currently sells more microprocessors than Intel.

3.3 MEMORY LAYOUT

Memory consists of a number of cells, each of which will hold one eight bit number or byte. Memory cells are numbered starting at zero up to the maximum allowable amount of memory (Figure 3.2). Programs consist of instructions and data. Careful organization is required to prevent the computer interpreting instructions as data or vice versa, since everything in the memory is stored as groups of bits.

The organization of memory in MIPS systems is conventional. A program's address space is composed of three parts (see Figure 3.3).

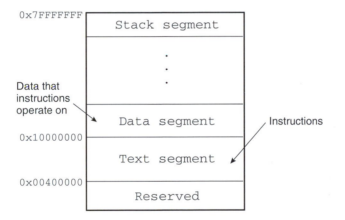

Figure 3.2 Memory organization.

Figure 3.3 MIPS memory layout.

At the bottom of the user address space (0x400000) is the text segment, which holds the instructions for a program. Above the text segment is the data segment, starting at 0x10000000. The stack is a last in, first out queue which is needed to implement procedures, allowing programmers to structure software to make it easier to understand and reuse (see Chapter 8). The program stack resides at the top of the address space (0x7fffffff). It grows down, towards the data segment.

3.4   THE MIPS REGISTERS

The processor's memory consists of a number of registers, each of which has a certain function. The most important register is the program counter (PC) which points to, or holds the memory address of, the next instruction to be executed.

The MIPS (and SPIM) processor contains 32 general purpose registers that are numbered 0–31. Register *n* is designated by $n, or R*n*. Register $0 always contains the hardwired value 0. MIPS has established a set of conventions as to how registers should be used. These suggestions are guidelines, which are not enforced by the hardware. However, a program that violates them will not work properly with other software. Table 3.1 lists the commonly used registers and describes their intended use. These MIPS registers, as seen using the XSPIM programming tool, are shown in Figure 4.5.

The conventions for the use of the registers will become clear when we study assembly language support for procedure calls in Chapter 8. Registers $at (1), $k0 (26) and $k1 (27) are reserved for use by the assembler and operating system. Registers $a0–$a3 (4–7) are used to pass the first four arguments to procedures (remaining arguments are passed on the stack). Registers $v0 and $v1 (2, 3) are used to return values from procedures. Registers $t0–$t9 (8–15, 24, 25) are called saved registers and are used for temporary quantities that do not need to be preserved when a procedure calls another that may also use these registers. In contrast, registers $s0–$s7 (16–23) are called saved registers and hold long-lived values that will need to be preserved across calls. Register $sp (29) is the stack pointer, which points to the last location in use on the stack. Register $fp (30) is the frame pointer. A procedure call frame is an area of memory used to hold various information associated with a procedure, such as arguments, saved registers and local variables, as discussed in Chapter 8. Register $ra (31) is written with the return address when a new procedure is called. Register $gp (28) is a global pointer that points into the middle of a 64K block of memory that holds constants and global variables. The objects in this part of memory can be quickly accessed with a single load or store instruction.

Table 3.1 MIPS registers and the convention governing their use.

Register name	Number	Usage
zero	$0	Constant 0
$at	$1	Reserved for assembler
$v0–$v1	$2–$3	Expression evaluation and results of a function
$a0–$a3	$4–$7	Argument 1–4
$t0–$t7	$8–$15	Temporary (not preserved across call)
$s0–$s7	$16–$23	Saved temporary (preserved across call)
$t8–$t9	$24–$25	Temporary (not preserved across call)
$k0–$k1	$26–$27	Reserved for OS kernel
$gp	$28	Pointer to global area
$sp	$29	Stack pointer
$fp	$30	Frame pointer
$ra	$31	Return address (used by function call)

The MIPS processor also has 16 floating point registers $f0...$f15 to hold numbers in floating point form, such as

$$3.459 \times 10^9$$

3.5 THE SPIM SIMULATOR

SPIM is a simulator that runs programs for the MIPS R2000/R3000 RISC computers. SPIM can read and immediately execute files containing assembly language. SPIM is a self-contained system for running these programs and contains a debugger and interface to a few operating system services.

There are many advantages to using a machine simulator like SPIM. MIPS workstations are not generally available, and these machines will not persist for many years because of the rapid progress leading to new and faster computers. Unfortunately, the trend to make computers faster by executing several instructions concurrently makes their architecture more difficult to understand and program in assembly language. Simulators can provide a better environment for low-level programming than an actual machine because they can detect more errors and provide more features than an actual computer.

One method frequently used to study assembly programming is a specially designed circuit board with a processor, memory and various I/O devices. The edit–assemble–load development cycle is much faster with a simulator than downloading assembly programs to a simple microprocessor system. In addition, such systems are prone to hardware problems, which means that the programmer is never sure whether a problem is a bug in the code or due to a hardware problem. With a simulator the possibility of this happening is removed, although there is always the possibility of bugs in the simulator software. Such bugs are easier to detect and fix than intermittent hardware failures.

SPIM has an X-Window interface that is better than most debuggers for the actual machines. The only disadvantage of a simulated machine is that the programs will run slower than on a real machine, although this is not a problem for testing simple workloads.

The Unix version of SPIM provides a simple terminal and an X-Window interface. Both provide equivalent functionality, but the X interface is generally easier to use and more informative. The simulator is available free to users. There are also Macintosh and PC versions of the simulator available in the public domain (see Preface).

3.6 I/O ORGANIZATION

This section explains how input and output (I/O) is organized by the SPIM simulator. A computer would be useless without low-level software running on it. The lowest level software on the computer is the operating system

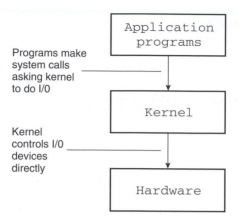

Figure 3.4 Operating system calls.

kernel. Among other things it knows the particular commands that each I/O device understands. An application program asks the kernel to do I/O by making a system call, as shown in Figure 3.4. The kernel implements these system calls by talking directly to the hardware. Typically, an operating system may have hundreds of system calls.

SPIM provides a small set of 10 operating-system-like services through the system call (`syscall`) instruction. In effect, these simulate an extremely simple operating system. To request a service, a program loads the system call code (see Table 3.2) into register $v0 and the arguments into registers $a0...$a3 (or $f12 for floating point values). System calls that return values put their result in register $v0 (or $f0 for floating point results). The use of these system calls will be explained and demonstrated in example programs in the following chapters. For example, `print_int` is passed an integer and prints it on the console. `print_float` prints a single floating point number. `read_int` reads an entire line of input up to and including the newline and returns an integer. Characters following the number are ignored. `exit` stops a program from running.

Table 3.2 SPIM's system calls.

Service	Call code	Arguments	Result
print_int	1	$a0 = integer	
print_float	2	$f12 = float	
print_double	3	$f12 = double	
print_string	4	$a0 = string	
read_int	5		integer (in $v0)
read_float	6		float (in $f0)
read_double	7		double (in $f0)
read_string	8	$a0 = buffer, $a1 = length	
sbrk	9	$a0 = amount	address (in $v0)
exit	10		

3.7 SUMMARY

RISC machines are based on the idea that by speeding up the commonest simple instructions one could afford to pay a penalty in the unusual case of more complex operations and make a large net gain in performance. Memory consists of a number of cells, each of which will hold one eight-bit number or byte. A program's address space is composed of three parts – the text segment, which holds the instructions for a program, the data segment and the stack segment. The MIPS processor contains 32 general-purpose registers and conventions have been established as to how registers should be used. An application program asks the kernel to do I/O by making system calls which the kernel implements by talking directly to the hardware. SPIM is a simulator that runs programs for the MIPS computers.

EXERCISES

3.1 What is the basic idea behind RISC processors?

3.2 What goes in a text segment?

3.3 What is the purpose of the program counter?

3.4 Discuss the advantages of simulated machines.

3.5 How is I/O organized in SPIM?

3.6 What is the number of the return address register?

CHAPTER 4

An example MIPS program

4.1 INTRODUCTION

This chapter begins by outlining the syntax used in a MIPS assembly language program. It then considers a simple example program. The instructions used in this program are introduced. The XSPIM programming tool is then described. Detailed instructions for executing the example program using XSPIM are given. Additional simple load, store and arithmetic instructions are introduced, together with some example programs illustrating their use.

4.2 SOURCE CODE FORMAT

An assembly program is usually held in a file with .a at the end of the filename, for example `hello.a`. This file is processed line by line by the SPIM program. Each line in the source code file can either translate into a machine instruction (or several machine instructions in the case of an assembly pseudo-instruction), can generate data element(s) to be stored in memory, or may provide information to the assembler program.

The file `hello.a` below contains the source code of a program to print out a character string. A string is an example of an array data structure – a named list of items stored in memory as shown in Figure 4.1. A character string is a contiguous sequence of ASCII bytes (Figure 2.8), with a byte whose value is zero used to indicate the end of the string. The following assembly program sets up a string in the data segment. The text segment contains instructions that make a system call to print out the string, followed by a system call to exit the program:

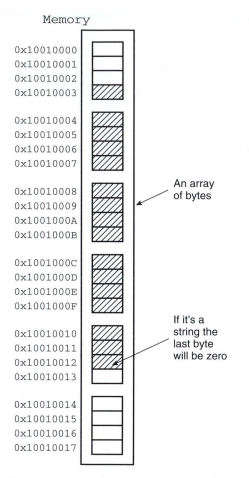

Figure 4.1 An array of bytes stored in memory.

```
 1    ##
 2    ## hello.a - prints out "hello world"
 3    ##
 4    ##      a0 - points to the string
 5    ##
 6
 7    #################################################
 8    #                                               #
 9    #                text segment                   #
10    #                                               #
11    #################################################
12
```

```
13              .text
14              .globl __start
15   __start:                    # execution starts here
16          la $a0,str           # put string address into a0
17          li $v0,4             # system call to print
18          syscall              # out a string
19
20          li $v0,10
21          syscall              # au revoir...
22
23
24   ##################################################
25   #                                                #
26   #               data segment                     #
27   #                                                #
28   ##################################################
29
30              .data
31   str:       .asciiz "hello world\n"
32
33   ##
34   ## end of file hello.a
```

Line numbers are only included in the program for the sake of clarity and are not entered when typing in programs. Information in the data segment does not contain instructions that are executed but rather is data used during program execution.

Regardless of the use of a particular line of the source code the format is relatively standard, divided into four fields separated by tabs as follows

```
[label:] operation [operand],[operand],[operand] [#comment]
```

It is extremely important in all languages, but especially in assembly language to indent the code properly using the tab or space keys to make the program as readable as possible, both by the author and others. Brackets ([ ]) indicate an optional field, so not all fields appear on each line. Comments are optional in the definition of the language, but must be sprinkled liberally in an assembly program to enhance readability. Depending on the particular operation and the needs of the program, a label and operand(s) may be required on a line.

4.2.1   COMMENTS

Comments in assembler files begin with a sharp sign (#). Everything from the sharp sign to the end of the line is ignored by the assembler. Since assembly language is not self-documenting it is a good idea to use a lot of comments in an assembly program, as the source code will otherwise be more difficult to read and understand than, say, a program written in a high-level language like C.

4.2.2 LABELS

Identifiers are a sequence of alphanumeric characters, underbars (_), and dots (.) that do not begin with a number, for example `str` in line 31 of `hello.a`. Opcodes for instructions, such as `la` of `li`, are reserved words that are not valid identifiers. Labels are declared by putting identifiers at the beginning of a line followed by a colon, as can be seen in both the text and data segments of `hello.a`. When choosing an identifier, it is a good idea to pick one which has a meaning that increases the readability of the program, for example `str` for the address of a string, rather than say `L59` for the fifty-ninth label! A programmer who uses meaningless labels at the time of coding will never get round to altering them, and will be unable to figure out the program in a few weeks' time. Often labels are kept to fewer than eight characters to facilitate the formatting of the source using tabs.

If a label is present, it is used to associate the symbol with the memory address of a variable, located in the data segment, or the address of an instruction in the text segment.

4.2.3 OPERATION FIELD

The operation field contains either a machine instruction or an assembler directive. Each machine instruction has a special symbol or mnemonic associated with it. The full set of SPIM mnemonics is listed in Appendix C. If a particular instruction is needed by the programmer, the corresponding mnemonic is placed in the operation field. For example, the `la` mnemonic is used in `hello.a` to cause the load address instruction to be placed at this point in the program.

The operation field can also hold an assembler directive, which does not translate into a machine instruction. In `hello.a` the directive `.data` is used to tell the assembler to place what follows in the data segment of the program.

4.2.4 OPERAND FIELD

Many machine instructions require one or more operands. For example, in `hello.a` register names, labels and numerical quantities are used as operands. Assembler directives may also require operand(s).

4.2.5   CONSTANTS

A constant is a value that does not change during program assembly or execution. Program hello.a uses both integer and character string constants. If an integer constant is specified without indicating its base, it is assumed to be a decimal number. To indicate a number in hexadecimal, prefix the number with 0x and use either lower- or upper-case letters: a-f or A-F.

A string constant is delimited by double quotes (") for example:

```
"hello world\n"
```

Special characters in strings follow the C convention:

```
newline          \n
tab              \t
quote            \"
```

SPIM supports two assembler directives for character strings.

```
.ascii "abcd"
```

stores the ASCII bytes in memory, but does not null-terminate them.

```
.asciiz  "abcd"
```

stores the string in memory and null-terminates it.

4.3   **DESCRIPTION OF** hello.a

The example program hello.a prints out the characters hello world. It is a very simple program which sets up the string in the data segment and makes a system call to print out this string in the text segment, followed by a system call to exit the program. After the initial comments, the

```
.text
```

directive (line 13) tells the assembler to place what follows in the text segment. The following two lines (lines 14–15)

```
.globl __start
```

```
__start:
```

attach the label __start to the first instruction so that the assembler can identify where execution should begin. All programs in this book will have these three lines unchanged.

As mentioned already, SPIM provides a small set of operating-system-like services through the system call (syscall) instruction. To request a service, a program loads the system call code (see Table 3.2) into register $v0 (for example, 10 = exit, 1 = print an integer, 4 = print a string, 5 = read an integer, etc.) and the arguments into registers $a0...$a3. To set up the system call it is necessary to load values into the registers. The la, or load address instruction (Figure 4.2) puts an address into a register (line 16). It takes two operands, the first being the register and the second being the address. Note the register names all begin with $.

The dagger (†) in the instruction set reference means that la is a pseudo-instruction. In order to make it easier to write, read and understand source code, assemblers provide some extra instructions which do not correspond to a single machine instruction but instead consist of a sequence of machine instructions. As we shall see shortly when we execute the program instruction by instruction, called single stepping, la requires two machine instructions, since the address is a 32-bit quantity, and is therefore a pseudo-instruction.

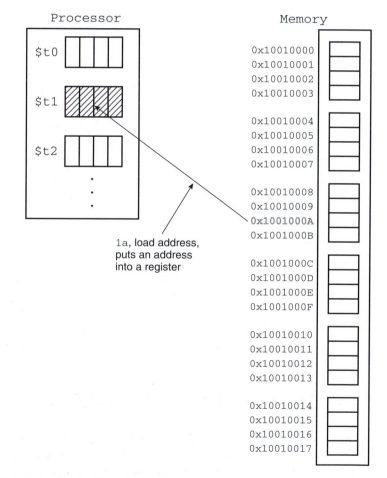

Figure 4.2 la: load address instruction.

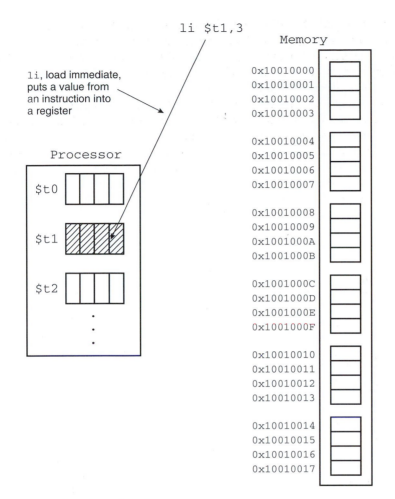

Figure 4.3 li: load immediate instructions.

li (Figure 4.3) is load immediate (line 17). Immediate means the processor extracts a value from the instruction itself, not from memory, and stores it in the register. If the size of the constant is limited to 16 bits this pseudo-instruction can fit in a single machine instruction. Load immediate takes two operands, the first being the register and the second being the number to be loaded.

4.4   PUTTING THEORY INTO PRACTICE

This section discusses the Unix version of SPIM. Versions for PC or Macintosh are almost identical. XSPIM is an X-Window application that implements a simulated MIPS environment. The environment allows assembling and debugging of assembly code written with the MIPS instruction set.

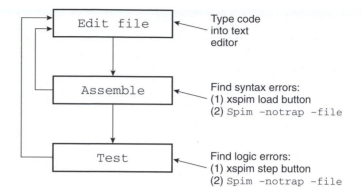

Figure 4.4   Edit, assemble and test cycle.

The basic method of programming with XSPIM is to have the XSPIM window open, and also an editor window open with the code you are working on. To test your code, you load it and run it in XSPIM. Usually you will encounter errors in your code, so you make changes to your code in your editor, save your code from your editor, clear the XSPIM environment, reload your code into XSPIM, and finally re-run your code in XSPIM. This cycle continues until you've removed all the bugs from your code. Figure 4.4 shows the steps involved in getting an assembly program to work.

4.4.1   STARTING XSPIM

To run XSPIM type `xspim -notrap &` and press enter. The `notrap` option is needed so that control will begin from the `__start` label in your program. When the XSPIM window comes up, note the division of the window: at the top the current states of all of the registers in the simulated machine are displayed (Figure 4.5). The values of these registers will change as you run your program. Below the registers are the control buttons (Figure 4.6), which are used to tell XSPIM what to do.

Next is the text segment, Figure 4.7, which is broken into these five columns (listed left to right):

- the address of the instruction
- the hex encoding of the instruction (machine language)
- the mnemonic description of the instruction, along with explicit register names and explicit addresses
- the line number of the code from your program
- the line of code from your program that produced this instruction. Note that the instruction in your code may not match exactly the instruction in the third column, because some MIPS instructions are actually pseudo-instructions, which may consist of several machine instructions.

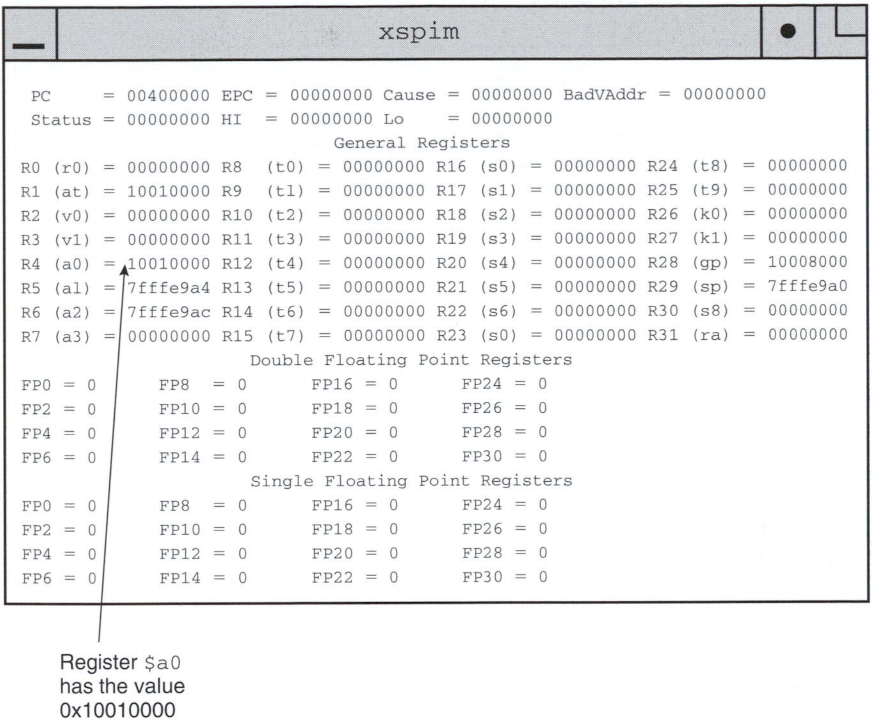

```
┌──┬─────────────────────────────────────────────────────────┬─────┬──┐
│──│                         xspim                           │  ●  │ └│
├──┴─────────────────────────────────────────────────────────┴─────┴──┤

  PC     = 00400000 EPC = 00000000 Cause = 00000000 BadVAddr = 00000000
  Status = 00000000 HI  = 00000000 Lo    = 00000000
                           General Registers
 R0 (r0) = 00000000 R8  (t0) = 00000000 R16 (s0) = 00000000 R24 (t8) = 00000000
 R1 (at) = 10010000 R9  (t1) = 00000000 R17 (s1) = 00000000 R25 (t9) = 00000000
 R2 (v0) = 00000000 R10 (t2) = 00000000 R18 (s2) = 00000000 R26 (k0) = 00000000
 R3 (v1) = 00000000 R11 (t3) = 00000000 R19 (s3) = 00000000 R27 (k1) = 00000000
 R4 (a0) = 10010000 R12 (t4) = 00000000 R20 (s4) = 00000000 R28 (gp) = 10008000
 R5 (a1) = 7fffe9a4 R13 (t5) = 00000000 R21 (s5) = 00000000 R29 (sp) = 7fffe9a0
 R6 (a2) = 7fffe9ac R14 (t6) = 00000000 R22 (s6) = 00000000 R30 (s8) = 00000000
 R7 (a3) = 00000000 R15 (t7) = 00000000 R23 (s0) = 00000000 R31 (ra) = 00000000
                      Double Floating Point Registers
  FP0  = 0      FP8  = 0      FP16 = 0      FP24 = 0
  FP2  = 0      FP10 = 0      FP18 = 0      FP26 = 0
  FP4  = 0      FP12 = 0      FP20 = 0      FP28 = 0
  FP6  = 0      FP14 = 0      FP22 = 0      FP30 = 0
                      Single Floating Point Registers
  FP0  = 0      FP8  = 0      FP16 = 0      FP24 = 0
  FP2  = 0      FP10 = 0      FP18 = 0      FP26 = 0
  FP4  = 0      FP12 = 0      FP20 = 0      FP28 = 0
  FP6  = 0      FP14 = 0      FP22 = 0      FP30 = 0
```

Register $a0
has the value
0x10010000

Figure 4.5 XSPIM view of current state of all of the registers in the simulated machine.

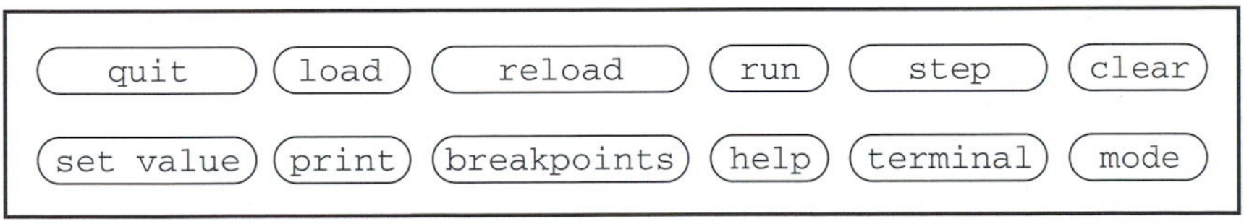

```
┌──────────────────────────────────────────────────────────────────┐
│  ( quit )  ( load )  (  reload  )  ( run )  ( step )  ( clear )    │
│                                                                    │
│  ( set value ) ( print ) ( breakpoints ) ( help ) ( terminal ) ( mode ) │
└──────────────────────────────────────────────────────────────────┘
```

Figure 4.6 Control buttons to tell XSPIM what to do.

Below the text segment is the data segment (Figure 4.8), where you can see the data portion of your code. The XSPIM tool prints out the data segment as if each four bytes represented a word. If the data in fact represents characters, the ASCII codes for four characters will appear in each word. The order of the bytes within a word will depend on the way the particular computer on which XSPIM is running has been built. At the very bottom of the XSPIM window is the messages area, where XSPIM gives you feedback, such as notifying you that your program crashed or alerting you to a malformed instruction.

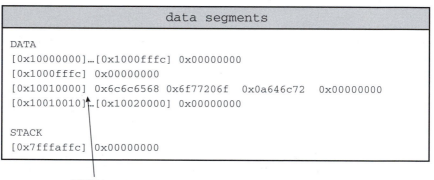

```
                      text  segments
[0x00400000] 0x3c011001 lui $1, 4097  [str]  ; 16: la $a0, # str put string addre

[0x00400004] 0x34200000 ori $4, $1, 0 [str]

[0x00400008] 0x34020004 ori $2, $0, 4      ; 17: li $v0, # system call to pri

[0x0040000c] 0x0000000c syscall            ; 18: syscall

[0x00400010] 0x3402000a ori $2, $0, 10     ; 20: li $v0, 10

[0x00400014] 0x0000000c syscall            ; 21: syscall
```

Highlighted
line is the
next to be
executed

Figure 4.7 Text segment broken into these five columns.

```
                      data  segments
DATA
[0x10000000]...[0x1000fffc] 0x00000000
[0x1000fffc] 0x00000000
[0x10010000] 0x6c6c6568 0x6f77206f  0x0a646c72  0x00000000
[0x10010010]...[0x10020000] 0x00000000

STACK
[0x7fffaffc] 0x00000000
```

ASCII 'hello
world' stored
at 0x10010000.
Note the order

Figure 4.8 Data segment of MIPS program.

4.4.2 LOADING AN ASSEMBLY PROGRAM

Once you have the XSPIM window open you need to load your program.
Press the 'load' button and, a window will come up (Figure 4.9) asking you
for a filename. Type in the name of your program and press 'assemble file'.
XSPIM will proceed to load and assemble your program. Look in the
message area of the XSPIM window for errors that XSPIM may have found
while assembling your program.

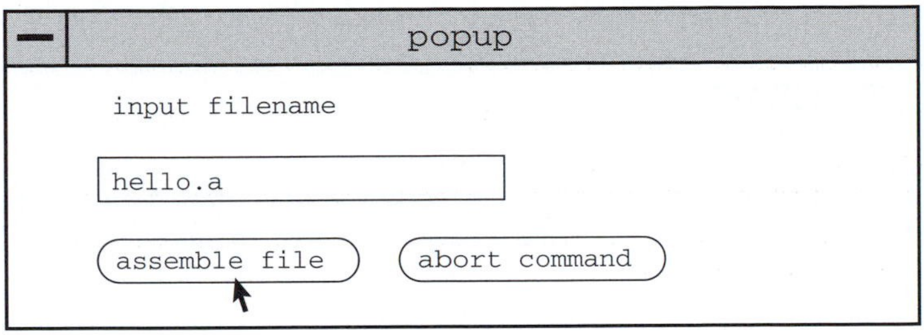

```
 ┌──┬────────────────────────────────────────────────┐
 │ ─│                    popup                        │
 ├──┴────────────────────────────────────────────────┤
 │                                                    │
 │      input filename                                │
 │                                                    │
 │      ┌──────────────────────────────┐              │
 │      │ hello.a                      │              │
 │      └──────────────────────────────┘              │
 │                                                    │
 │     ( assemble file )    ( abort command )         │
 │              ↑                                     │
 │                                                    │
 └────────────────────────────────────────────────────┘
```

Figure 4.9   Window used to load a file in XSPIM.

It is also possible to use the command line interface to the SPIM program by typing `spim -notrap -file` followed by the filename, which will show any syntax errors in a terminal window.

4.4.3   EXECUTING AN ASSEMBLY PROGRAM

Once your program has successfully loaded (meaning **XSPIM** found the file and did not encounter any errors while assembling it) you can run it. First, press the 'terminal' button and pull-down to 'popup console', which will bring up another window that will display any output the program produces. To run your program press the 'Run' button (Figure 4.10). You will be asked for the address at which you wish XSPIM to begin executing. The default address should be correct, so press the 'ok' button and your program will run.

If your program didn't seem to work properly, look at the messages portion of the window for hints from **XSPIM** as to what the problem is.

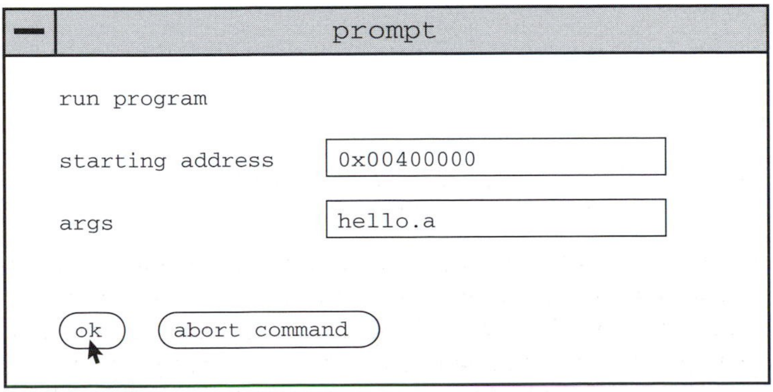

```
 ┌──┬────────────────────────────────────────────────┐
 │ ─│                    prompt                       │
 ├──┴────────────────────────────────────────────────┤
 │                                                    │
 │    run program                                     │
 │                                                    │
 │                          ┌────────────────────┐    │
 │    starting address      │ 0x00400000         │    │
 │                          └────────────────────┘    │
 │                          ┌────────────────────┐    │
 │    args                  │ hello.a            │    │
 │                          └────────────────────┘    │
 │                                                    │
 │   ( ok )  ( abort command )                        │
 │       ↑                                            │
 └────────────────────────────────────────────────────┘
```

Figure 4.10   Window used to run a program in XSPIM.

4.4.4 RELOADING AND RE-EXECUTING AN ASSEMBLY PROGRAM

Usually your program won't work perfectly the first time. You will no doubt observe changes to your code that you would like to make. Once you have modified your code in your editor (which it is assumed you have open along with XSPIM), press the 'clear' button on the XSPIM window and pull it down to 'memory & registers'. This will clear the state of the simulated machine so that you can run the fresh new version of your program. Now press 'load' and XSPIM remembers the filename of your program, so just press 'assembly file' and XSPIM will reload it. Finally, press 'run' and then 'ok' to re-execute your program.

4.4.5 DEBUGGING AN ASSEMBLY PROGRAM

Syntax errors are easy to locate and fix because the assembler will automatically tell you the line number which caused the problem. Single stepping is extremely important because it is the best way to find a logical error in your program by pinpointing the precise line which caused the error. Debugging with XSPIM usually amounts to single stepping through each instruction in your program and observing the changes in the state of the registers. The particular line that the program counter has reached is highlighted in the text segment window as the processor stops during execution. This method exposes most bugs quickly. To step through your program you must either declare a breakpoint or start stepping from the __start label line by line. A breakpoint is a spot in your program where XSPIM will temporarily suspend execution so that you may view the suspended state of the simulated machine. After observing the state, you may tell XSPIM to finish executing your program in its entirety (or until it encounters another breakpoint), or you may step through your program line by line. Breakpoints are useful to pass over a loop quickly and avoid single stepping around it many times.

Single stepping control

To continue execution of your program from a breakpoint, or at the very start of your program, press the 'step' button. This brings up the step window (Figure 4.11), which allows you to either step through your program (press the 'step' button) or continue execution of your program (press the 'continue' button).

Setting a breakpoint

To set a breakpoint you must first observe the address of the instruction where you wish to suspend execution (remember, the address is the first column of the text segment in the XSPIM window). Next, press the

```
┌─────────────────────────────────────────────────────────────┐
│ ─ │                    prompt                                 │
├─────────────────────────────────────────────────────────────┤
│                                                              │
│   step program                                               │
│   number of steps                                            │
│                        ┌──────────────────────────────┐      │
│                        │ 1                            │      │
│                        └──────────────────────────────┘      │
│   args                                                       │
│                        ┌──────────────────────────────┐      │
│                        │ hello.a                      │      │
│                        └──────────────────────────────┘      │
│                                                              │
│                                                              │
│   ( step )    ( continue )      ( abort command )            │
│                                                              │
└─────────────────────────────────────────────────────────────┘
```

Figure 4.11   Window used to single step in XSPIM.

```
┌─────────────────────────────────────────────────────────────┐
│ ─ │                    popup                                  │
├─────────────────────────────────────────────────────────────┤
│                                                              │
│   address                                                    │
│   ┌────────────────────────────────┐                         │
│   │ 0x00400008                    │                         │
│   └────────────────────────────────┘                         │
│   ( add )  ( delete )  ( list )   ( abort command )          │
│                                                              │
└─────────────────────────────────────────────────────────────┘
```

Figure 4.12   Window used to set a breakpoint in XSPIM.

'Breakpoints' button (Figure 4.12), then type in the address of the breakpoint and press 'add'. When you run your program, XSPIM will suspend execution at the breakpoint that you specified. Note that it is possible to set multiple breakpoints. The breakpoints window (press the 'breakpoints' button from the XSPIM window) allows you to maintain a list of breakpoints.

4.5   LOAD AND STORE INSTRUCTIONS

lw (Figure 4.13) and sw are load and store word instructions – they load words from memory into registers, and store words into memory from registers. There is also a version that works on bytes – lb and sb (Figure 4.14). Note the requirement for alignment; the memory address associated with lw or sw must be a multiple of four because of the way memory is built.

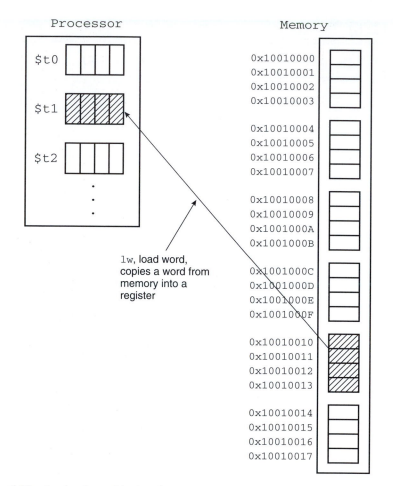

Figure 4.13 lw: load word instruction.

4.6 ARITHMETIC INSTRUCTIONS

All arithmetic (and logical) instructions take three operands. The mnemonic

```
add $t0,$t1,$t2
```

means

```
t0 = t1 + t2
```

Note the order of the operands. The arguments are the contents of the registers, so this is known as register addressing mode. A programmer who needs one input to be a constant can use:

```
addi $t0,$t1,15
```

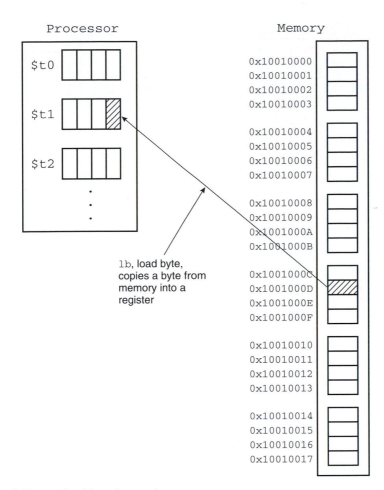

Figure 4.14 `lb`: load byte instruction.

This instruction is called 'add immediate' because the constant is stored in the actual instruction, and is immediately available to the processor without having to access memory. Different addressing modes will be discussed in more detail in Chapter 6.

In the instruction references, Appendix B and Appendix C, Rdest and Rsrc mean registers used as the destination and source operands. Src means either a register or a constant used as an operand. So, for example, the format listed for add is

        add Rdest,Rsrc1,Src2

which means the destination and first operand must be registers, but the second operand can be either a register or a constant. If you type

        add $t0,$t1,15

the assembler will automatically generate an `addi` instruction for you. Also, if you only give one register the assembler will assume you wish to add the constant to that register. Thus

```
add $t0,17
```

means

```
addi $t0,$t0,17
```

4.7   MULTIPLICATION AND DIVISION

The actual MIPS instruction is `mult Rs,Rt`, which means multiply contents of Rs by contents of Rt. Since the result of multiplying two *n*-bit numbers can be up to *2n* bits, MIPS uses two special registers, called `lo` and `hi`, to hold the results of multiplications. Special move instructions copy data from general registers (`r0..r31`) to/from `lo` and `hi`. You don't have to worry too much about the details of this. The pseudo-instruction `mul Rdest,Rsrc1,Src2` will assemble into the real instructions to do the multiply.

```
mul $t4,$t4,$t1
```

is the same as

```
mult $t4,$t1
mflo $t4              move from the lo register
```

Similarly, there is a `div Rdest,Rsrc1,Src2` pseudo-instruction to do integer division. Program `dec.a` on pp. 78–80 will provide an example of its usage. Table 4.1 summarizes the usage of the MIPS processor's arithmetic instructions.

Table 4.1   Examples of MIPS arithmetic instructions.

Instruction	Example	
Add	`add $t1,$t2,$t3`	`# $t1=$t2+$t3`
Add immediate	`addi $t1,$t2,50`	`# $t1=$t2+50`
Subtract	`sub $t1,$t2,$t3`	`# $t1=$t2-$t3`
Multiply	`mult $t2,$t3`	`# Hi,Lo=$t2x$t3`
Divide	`div $t2,$t3`	`# Lo=$t2÷$t3,` `# Hi=$t2 mod $t3`
Move from Hi	`mfhi $t1`	`# $t1=Hi` `# get copy of Hi`
Move from Lo	`mflo $t1`	`# $t1=Lo` `# get copy of Lo`

The program `temp.a` asks a user for a temperature in Celsius, converts it to Fahrenheit, and prints the result.

```
 1    ##
 2    ## temp.a ask user for temperature in Celsius,
 3    ##  convert to Fahrenheit, print the result.
 4    ##
 5    ##       v0 - reads in celsius
 6    ##       t0 - holds Fahrenheit result
 7    ##       a0 - points to output strings
 8    ##
 9
10    ###################################################
11    #                                                 #
12    #                 text segment                    #
13    #                                                 #
14    ###################################################
15
16            .text
17            .globl __start
18    __start:
19            la $a0,prompt     # print prompt on terminal
20            li $v0,4
21            syscall
22
23            li $v0,5          # syscall 5 reads an integer
24            syscall
25
26            mul $t0,$v0,9     # to convert,multiply by 9,
27            div $t0,$t0,5     # divide by 5,then
28            add $t0,$t0,32    # add 32
29
30            la $a0,ans1       # print string before result
31            li $v0,4
32            syscall
33
34            move $a0,$t0      # print  result
35            li $v0,1
36            syscall
37
38            la $a0,endl       # system call to print
39            li $v0,4          # out a newline
40            syscall
41
42            li $v0,10
43            syscall           # au revoir...
```

```
44
45
46      ##################################################
47      #                                                #
48      #              data segment                      #
49      #                                                #
50      ##################################################
51
52              .data
53              prompt: .asciiz "Enter temperature (Celsius): "
54              ans1:   .asciiz "The temperature in Fahrenheit is
55              endl:   .asciiz "\n"
56
57              ##
58              ## end of file temp.a
```

temp.a is interesting because it uses syscall five to read in an integer (line 23) that should be a Celsius temperature. It uses the `mul` pseudo-instruction (line 26) and the `div` pseudo-instruction (line 27) to work out the temperature in Fahrenheit. When writing code for the automatically correcting system (Appendix A), it is important not to use syscall five to read in input. The data for such programs will always be stored in the data segment.

4.8 PROGRAMMING EXAMPLE

math1.a below is a programming question that tests knowledge of the arithmetic instructions together with the load word instruction. The question is in the input format for the automatic testing system described fully in Appendix A.

Note: Whenever you see a 'skeleton' file such as math1.a in this book, you should attempt to write the program asked for in the opening lines of the file in the space provided between the dashed lines.

```
1    ## Start of file math1.a
2    ##
3    ## Question:
4    ## calculate A*X^2+B*X+C
5    ##
6    ## Output format must be:
7    ## "answer = 180"
```

```
 8
 9     ##################################################
10     #                                                #
11     #                text segment                    #
12     #                                                #
13     ##################################################
14
15              .text
16              .globl __start
17       __start:                    # execution starts here
18
19
20     # Any changes above this line will be discarded by
21     # mipsmark. Put your answer between dashed lines.
22     #------------ start cut -------------------------
23
24
25
26     #------------  end cut  -------------------------
27     # Any changes below this line will be discarded by
28     # mipsmark. Put your answer between dashed lines.
29
30     ##################################################
31     #                                                #
32     #                data segment                    #
33     #                                                #
34     ##################################################
35
36              .data
37     X:       .word 7
38     A:       .word 3
39     B:       .word 4
40     C:       .word 5
41     ans:     .asciiz "answer = "
42     endl:    .asciiz "\n"
43     ##
44     ## End of file math1.a
```

Here is an attempted solution to the question, which contains a logical error. This section shows how to use source-level debugging to single step through the code and locate the error in the solution.

```
 1     # Any changes above this line will be discarded by
 2     # mipsmark. Put your answer between dashed lines.
 3     #------------ start cut -------------------------
```

```
 4
 5
 6    # solution to math1.a NOTE IT CONTAINS A BUG!!!!
 7
 8            lw $t0,X
 9            lw $t1,A
10            lw $t2,B
11            lw $t3,C
12
13            mul $t4,$t0,$t0 # t4 = X^2
14            mul $t4,$t4,$t1 # t4 = A*X^2
15            mul $t5,$2,$t0  # t5 = B*X
16            add $t4,$t4,$t5 # t4 = A*X^2+B*X
17            add $t4,$t4,$t3 # t4 = A*X^2+B*X+C
18
19            la $a0,ans      # system call to print
20            li $v0,4        # out string
21            syscall
22
23            move $a0,$t4    # print result on terminal
24            li $v0,1
25            syscall
26
27            la $a0,endl     # system call to print
28            li $v0,4        # out a newline
29            syscall
30
31            li $v0,10
32            syscall         # au revoir...
33
34    ##------------ end cut  -------------------------
35    # Any changes below this line will be discarded by
36    # mipsmark. Put your answer between dashed lines.
```

This attempted solution used the lw instruction to get the values of A, B, C and X into registers from memory (lines 8–11) so that the arithmetic instructions can be used to calculate the required result (lines 13–17). Lines 23–25 use syscall one to print the value of an integer.

The solution also uses the move pseudo-instruction (line 23) to move a value from one register to another so that the answer will be in $a0 for the system call. This is a good example of how an assembler can hide a messy machine detail from programmers.

```
    move $t0,$t1
```

means copy the contents of $t1 to $t0. MIPS does not have a move instruction in the machine language. But it does have an add, and it has a register $0 that always has the value zero, a very common constant. Machine language programmers who want to copy t1 to t0 would write the equivalent of

```
add $t0,$t1,$0
```

but the assembly language programmer can write move and have the assembler translate it into add.

If the above attempted solution is run, the answer printed out is 152, not the expected 180. The best way to find the bug is to load the program into the XSPIM tool and single step through it watching the values in the registers as each instruction is executed. Figure 4.15 shows XSPIM after the 'step' button has been pressed four times, corresponding to the first four machine instructions, or the first two assembly language pseudo-instructions. The correct values can be seen in the registers.

If the step button is repeatedly pressed, everything goes according to plan until the program counter reaches 0x00400030 (Figure 4.16), when it becomes clear that the programmer has inadvertently typed $2 instead of $t2. It is easy to alter this in a text editor, and clear and reload XSPIM, after which the program will function correctly.

Program counter \   X has gone into $t0   A has gone into $t1

```
PC      = 00400010    EPC   = 00000000    Cause = 00000000
Status  = 00000000    HI    = 00000000    Lo    = 00000000
                         General Registers
R0  (r0) = 00000000 R8  (t0) = 00000007 R16 (s0) = 00000000 R24 (t8) = 00000000
R1  (at) = 10010000 R9  (t1) = 00000003 R17 (s1) = 00000000 R25 (t9) = 00000000
R2  (v0) = 00000000 R10 (t2) = 00000000 R18 (s2) = 00000000 R26 (k0) = 00000000
R3  (v1) = 00000000 R11 (t3) = 00000000 R19 (s3) = 00000000 R27 (k1) = 00000000
R4  (a0) = 00000001 R12 (t4) = 00000000 R20 (s4) = 00000000 R28 (gp) = 10008000
R5  (a1) = 7fffeaf4 R13 (t5) = 00000000 R21 (s5) = 00000000 R29 (sp) = 7fffeffc
R6  (a2) = 7fffeafc R14 (t6) = 00000000 R22 (s6) = 00000000 R30 (s8) = 00000000
R7  (a3) = 00000000 R15 (t7) = 00000000 R23 (s7) = 00000000 R31 (ra) = 00000000

[0x00400000] 0x3c011001 lui  $1,  4097     [X]   ; 24: lw $t0,X
[0x00400004] 0x8c280000 lw   $8   0($1)    [X]
[0x00400008] 0x3c011001 lui  $1,  4097     [A]   ; 25: lw $t1,A
[0x0040000c] 0x8c290004 lw   $9,  4($1)    [A]
[0x00400010] 0x3c011001 lui  $1,  4097     [B]   ; 26: lw $t2,B
[0x00400014] 0x8c2a0008 lw   $10, 8($1)    [B]
[0x00400018] 0x3c011001 lui  $1,  4097     [C]   ; 27: lw $t3,C
[0x0040001c] 0x8c2b000c lw   $11, 12,($1)  [C]
```

Figure 4.15 XSPIM after the first two assembly language instructions.

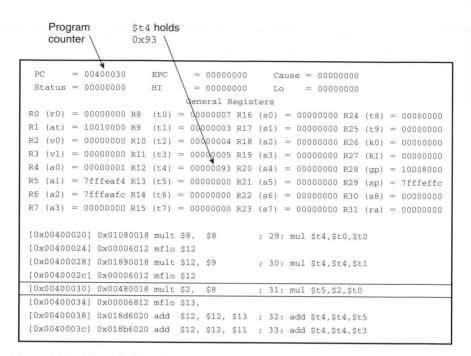

Figure 4.16 XSPIM when the bug is reached.

Two more example programs that test your understanding of the arithmetic instructions are math2.a and math3.a.

```
1     ## Start of file math2.a
2     ##
3     ## Question:
4     ## calculate 5*X^2-3
5     ##
6     ## Output format must be:
7     ## "answer = 242"
8
9     ################################################
10    #                                              #
11    #              text segment                    #
12    #                                              #
13    ################################################
14
15            .text
16            .globl __start
17    __start:               # execution starts here
18
19
```

```
20    # Any changes above this line will be discarded by
21    # mipsmark. Put your answer between dashed lines.
22    #------------ start cut -------------------------
23
24
25
26    #------------ end cut   -------------------------
27    # Any changes below this line will be discarded by
28    # mipsmark. Put your answer between dashed lines.
29
30    ################################################
31    #                                              #
32    #                data segment                  #
33    #                                              #
34    ################################################
35
36            .data
37    X:      .word 7
38    ans:    .asciiz "answer = "
39    endl:   .asciiz "\n"
40    ##
41    ## End of file math2.a

 1    ## Start of file math3.a
 2    ##
 3    ## Question:
 4    ## calculate (NUM-3)*(NUM+4)
 5    ##
 6    ## Output format must be:
 7    ## "answer = 98"
 8
 9    ################################################
10    #                                              #
11    #                text segment                  #
12    #                                              #
13    ################################################
14
15            .text
16            .globl __start
17    __start:                # execution starts here
18
19
20    # Any changes above this line will be discarded by
21    # mipsmark. Put your answer between dashed lines.
22    #------------ start cut -------------------------
23
```

```
24
25
26    #------------ end cut  -------------------------
27    # Any changes below this line will be discarded by
28    # mipsmark. Put your answer between dashed lines.
29
30    ##################################################
31    #                                                #
32    #               data segment                     #
33    #                                                #
34    ##################################################
35
36           .data
37    NUM:    .word 10
38    ans:    .asciiz "answer = "
39    endl:   .asciiz "\n"
40    ##
41    ## End of file math3.a
```

4.9 SUMMARY

Regardless of the use of a particular line of the assembly source code the format is relatively standard, divided into four fields separated by tabs. It is extremely important to indent the code properly using the tab key and to add comments liberally to make the program as readable as possible. In order to make it easier to write, read and understand source code, assemblers provide some extra pseudo-instructions which do not correspond exactly to a single machine instruction, but instead consist of a sequence of machine instructions. All arithmetic and logical instructions take three operands.

EXERCISES

4.1 What are the SPIM rules for forming identifiers?

4.2 What is the difference between a syntax error and a logical error?

4.3 What is the purpose of single stepping?

4.4 What is a breakpoint?

4.5 What are the hi and lo registers used for?

4.6 Why are comments and indentation so important in assembly language?

4.7 Describe the differences between la, lb, li and lw.

4.8 In what order should the operands of arithmetic and logical instructions be placed?

CHAPTER 5

Control flow structures

5.1 INTRODUCTION

This chapter looks at a program `length.a` that uses a program loop to work out the length of a character string. Familiarity with a few assembly language instructions, such as basic load, store and simple arithmetic operations is needed, together with the concept of program loops. A program loop allows an operation to be repeated a number of times, without having to enter the assembly language instructions explicitly. For example, to sum 50 numbers, one would not have 50 add instructions in the program, but instead would have the add instruction once and go round a loop 50 times.

5.2 CONTROL STRUCTURES

In an abstract view, operations in programs can be divided into two groups:

- data manipulation – expression evaluation and assignments
- control – determine which instruction to execute next.

From this point of view, all the action takes place in the assignments and the control instructions are just there to help the computer get the data manipulation instructions in the right order. The instructions used to alter the flow of control are known as branches and jumps. A branch specifies the number of instructions above or below the present instruction to move the program counter, whereas a jump specifies the actual address to move the PC to.

The simplest control instruction jump

```
j <addr>
```

means jump to address `<addr>` which causes the processor to fetch the next instruction from the word at address `<addr>`. Implementation is actually very simple – just copy the value of the address to the program counter. An alternative form of the jump instruction is

```
jr Rsrc
```

which means jump to the address held in register `Rsrc`.

5.3   CONDITIONAL BRANCHES

The jump instruction is also known as an unconditional jump, meaning that the processor always goes to the jump target address. Interesting programs need a way to make conditional branches. The MIPS conditional branch instructions have names that begin with `b` (`b` is for branches and `j` for jumps). Examples:

```
beq  $t0,$t1,<addr>     branch to <addr> if $t0 == $t1
beqz $t0,<addr>         branch to <addr> if $t0 == 0
bne  $t0,$t1,<addr>     branch to <addr> if $t0 != $t1
blt  $t0,$t1,<addr>     branch to <addr> if $t0 < $t1
```

and many more as listed in Appendix B, p. 146. Many of the branch instructions are pseudo-instructions, that is they are implemented by the assembler but don't correspond to actual machine instructions. The 'set on less than' instruction (Table 5.1) is used to implement some conditional branch pseudo-instructions. For example,

```
bge $t4,$t2,notMin
```

would look like

```
slt $1,$12,$10
beq $1,$0,8 [notMin-0x00400028]
```

For this scheme to work, the assembler needs to have a temporary register that it knows is not holding any useful data. By convention, that register is `$1`, also known as `$at`, the assembler temporary register. Don't put any variables in `$1` (at least not if you plan to use `blt` or any of the other branching pseudo-instructions). The assembler also helps out on branch instructions by letting the second operand be either a register or a constant. The 'branch on less than or equal' pseudo-instruction:

```
ble Rsrc,Src,addr
```

Table 5.1 Examples of MIPS jump, branch and compare instructions

Instruction	Example	
Branch on equal	`beq $t1,$t2,80`	`# if ($t1 == $t2)` `#     go to PC+4+80`
Branch on not equal	`bne $t1,$t2,-36`	`# if ($t1 != $t2)` `#     go to PC+4-36`
Set less than	`slt $t1,$t2,$t3`	`# if ($t2 < $t3) $t1=1` `# else $t1=0`
Set less than immediate	`slti $t1,$t2,7`	`# if ($t2 < 7) $t1=1` `# else $t1=0`
Jump	`j 0x00400068`	`# go to 0x00400068`
Jump register	`jr $ra`	`# go to $ra`
Jump and link	`jal 0x00400014`	`# $ra = PC + 4` `# go to 0x00400014`

can take a constant as one operand, for example,

```
ble $t0,5,loop
```

means branch to `loop` if `$t0` holds a number less than or equal to 5. Table 5.1 lists the usage of some of the MIPS processor's jump, branch and compare instructions.

5.4   EXAMPLE PROGRAMS USING LOOPS

The program `length.a` prints out the length of character string `str`:

```
 1    ##
 2    ## length.a - prints out the length of character
 3    ## string "str".
 4    ##
 5    ##      t0 - holds each byte from string in turn
 6    ##      t1 - contains count of characters
 7    ##      t2 - points to the string
 8    ##
 9
10    ##############################################
11    #                                            #
12    #               text segment                 #
13    #                                            #
14    ##############################################
```

```
15
16              .text
17              .globl __start
18  __start:                    # execution starts here
19          la $t2,str          # t2 points to the string
20          li $t1,0            # t1 holds the count
21  nextCh: lb $t0,($t2)        # get a byte from string
22          beqz $t0,strEnd     # zero means end of string
23          add $t1,$t1,1       # increment count
24          add $t2,1           # move pointer one character
25          j nextCh            # go round the loop again
26
27  strEnd: la $a0,ans          # system call to print
28          li $v0,4            # out a message
29          syscall
30
31          move $a0,$t1        # system call to print
32          li $v0,1            # out the length worked out
33          syscall
34
35          la $a0,endl         # system call to print
36          li $v0,4            # out a newline
37          syscall
38
39          li $v0,10
40          syscall             # au revoir...
41
42
43  ##################################################
44  #                                                #
45  #                data segment                    #
46  #                                                #
47  ##################################################
48
49              .data
50  str:        .asciiz "hello world"
51  ans:        .asciiz "Length is "
52  endl:       .asciiz "\n"
53
54  ##
55  ## end of file length.a
```

The character string in length.a is situated in memory, so the program must use the lb instruction (line 21) to bring characters in from memory to a register until it finds the zero byte that determines the end of the string, as shown in Figure 4.14. The ($t2) register is used to hold the memory address of the bytes in the string. Line 21 uses an addressing mode known as indirect addressing because we are not loading the value in the register, but rather using the value in the register as the address of the byte to load. The brackets () indicate indirect addressing. Register $t2 is sometimes called a pointer to the array of characters, since it holds the address of the quantity of interest. The add instruction is needed to move the pointer $a0 along the string (that is, add one to it), looking for the zero byte that signifies the end (line 24). add is also used to increment the count of characters in the string held in register $t1 (line 23). length.a uses the beqz, 'branch on equal zero' pseudo-instruction, line 22 to branch conditionally to the instruction at the label strEnd (line 27) if the contents of $t0 equals zero, signifying the end of the string, as shown in Figure 4.1. An unconditional jump (line 25) is used to return to the label nextCh (line 21) repeatedly progressing to the next character in the string. This assembly language program could be a while statement in a high-level language.

Another interesting example programming question that will add to your understanding of the conditional branching and program loops is loop3.a.

```
 1    ## Start of file loop3.a
 2    ##
 3    ## Question:
 4    ## Replace all occurrences of 'a' with
 5    ## 'A' in the string "chararray" and
 6    ## print the resulting string.
 7    ##
 8    ## Output format must be:
 9    ## "AbbbAAbbbAbAbAb"
10
11    ###############################################
12    #                                             #
13    #               text segment                  #
14    #                                             #
15    ###############################################
16
17            .text
18            .globl __start
19    __start:                    # execution starts here
20
21
22    # Any changes above this line will be discarded by
23    # mipsmark. Put your answer between dashed lines.
24    #----------- start cut ------------------------
```

```
25
26
27              la $t2,chararray# t2 points to the string
28              li $t1,'A'
29   nextCh: lb $t0,($t2)     # get a byte from string
30              beqz $t0,strEnd # zero means end of string
31              bne $t0,'a',nota
32              sb $t1,($t2)     # store upper case A
33   nota:    add $t2,1         # move pointer one character
34              j nextCh         # go round the loop again
35
36   strEnd:
37              la $a0,chararray
38              li $v0,4
39              syscall          # print
40
41              li $v0,10
42              syscall          # au revoir...
43
44   #------------ end cut  --------------------------
45   # Any changes below this line will be discarded by
46   # mipsmark. Put your answer between dashed lines.
47
48   ##################################################
49   #                                                #
50   #              data segment                      #
51   #                                                #
52   ##################################################
53
54              .data
55   chararray:
56              .asciiz "abbbaabbbababab\n"
57
58   ##
59   ## End of file loop3.a
```

In this program the bne instruction (line 31) is used to ensure that an upper-case A is only stored to memory when the character in that position was a lower case a. This would be an if statement in a high-level language. Note that 'A' in line 28 is used to mean the ASCII code for a letter. Line 32 uses the sb, store byte, instruction (Figure 5.1) to write a value from a register to the string in memory. Examples of the use of the other conditional instructions will be seen in other programs in subsequent chapters.

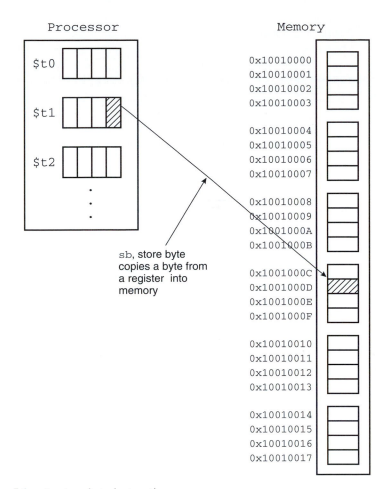

Figure 5.1 sb: store byte instruction.

Two more programs that test your understanding of these instructions
are loop4.a and loop5.a.

```
1    ## Start of file loop4.a
2    ##
3    ## Question:
4    ## Swap each pair of elements in
5    ## the string "chararray" and
6    ## print the resulting string.
7    ## There will always be an even number
8    ## of characters in "chararray".
9    ##
```

```
10      ## Output format must be:
11      ## "badcfe"
12
13      ###################################################
14      #                                                 #
15      #                 text segment                    #
16      #                                                 #
17      ###################################################
18
19              .text
20              .globl __start
21      __start:                    # execution starts here
22
23
24      # Any changes above this line will be discarded by
25      # mipsmark. Put your answer between dashed lines.
26      #------------ start cut --------------------------
27
28
29
30      #------------ end cut  ---------------------------
31      # Any changes below this line will be discarded by
32      # mipsmark. Put your answer between dashed lines.
33
34      ###################################################
35      #                                                 #
36      #                 data segment                    #
37      #                                                 #
38      ###################################################
39
40              .data
41      chararray:
42              .asciiz "abcdef"
43      endl:   .asciiz "\n"
44
45      ##
46      ## End of file loop4.a



1       ## Start of file loop5.a
2       ##
3       ## Question:
4       ## Replace every second character in the
5       ## string "charstr" with 'X'. That is
6       ## the first, third, fifth etc.
```

```
 7    ## There will always be an even number
 8    ## of characters in "charstr".
 9    ##
10    ## Then print the resulting string.
11    ##
12    ## Output format must be:
13    ## "XbXdXf"
14
15    #################################################
16    #                                               #
17    #                text segment                   #
18    #                                               #
19    #################################################
20
21            .text
22            .globl __start
23    __start:                    # execution starts here
24
25
26    # Any changes above this line will be discarded by
27    # mipsmark. Put your answer between dashed lines.
28    #------------ start cut --------------------------
29
30
31
32    #------------  end cut   -------------------------
33    # Any changes below this line will be discarded by
34    # mipsmark. Put your answer between dashed lines.
35
36    #################################################
37    #                                               #
38    #                data segment                   #
39    #                                               #
40    #################################################
41
42            .data
43    charstr:
44            .asciiz "abcdef"
45    endl:   .asciiz "\n"
46    ##
47    ## End of file loop5.a
```

Further programs to test your understanding of program loops are in Appendix A.3.

5.5 SUMMARY

All the action in an assembly language program takes place in the assignments, and the control instructions are just there to help the computer get the data manipulation instructions in the right order. A program loop allows an operation to be repeated a number of times, without having to enter the assembly language instructions explicitly. A branch specifies the number of instructions above or below the present instruction to move the program counter, whereas a jump specifies the actual address to move the program counter to. An unconditional jump means that the processor always goes to the jump target address, but interesting programs need a way to make conditional branches as well.

EXERCISES

5.1 What do control instructions do?

5.2 What is a conditional branch?

5.3 How does a loop determine the end of a character string?

5.4 Describe the indirect addressing mode.

5.5 What is a pointer?

5.6 What assembly language instructions does a compiler use to implement a while loop?

5.7 How are ASCII character codes loaded into registers in MIPS assembly?

CHAPTER 6

Addressing modes

6.1 INTRODUCTION

For any given operation, such as load, add or branch, there are often many different ways to specify the address of the operand(s). The different ways of determining the address are called addressing modes. This chapter looks at the different addressing modes of the MIPS processor and shows how all instructions can fit into a single four-byte word. Some sample programs are included to show additional addressing modes in action.

6.2 MIPS INSTRUCTION FORMATS

Every MIPS instruction consists of a single 32-bit word aligned on a word boundary. There are three different instruction formats: I type, R type and J type as, shown in Figure 6.1. The parts of each format have the following meaning:

- `op` – 6 bit operation code
- `rs` – 5 bit source register specifier
- `rd` – 5 bit destination register specifier
- `rt` – 5 bit target (source/destination) register or branch condition
- `immediate` – 16 bit immediate branch displacement or address displacement
- `target` – 26 bit jump target address
- `shamt` – 5 bit shift amount
- `funct` – 6 bit function field.

Register type

6	5	5	5	5	6
op Operation code	rs Source register specifier	rt Target register specifier	rd Destination register specifier	shamt Shift amount	funct Function field

Immediate type

6	5	5	16
op Operation code	rs Source register specifier	rt Target register specifier or branch condition	immediate Immediate, branch displacement or address displacement

Jump type

6	26
op Operation code	target Target address

Figure 6.1 MIPS instruction formats.

We have already seen examples of four different MIPS addressing modes while considering the programs hello.a and length.a. These are:

- register addressing mode
- base addressing mode
- immediate addressing mode
- PC-relative addressing mode.

In the following sections, we will examine each of these modes, observe how they are implemented using the above formats and introduce indexed addressing mode, which is implemented by the assembler as a pseudo-instruction.

6.3 MIPS REGISTER ADDRESSING

Register addressing (Figure 6.2) is the simplest addressing mode. Instructions using registers execute quickly because they avoid the delays associated with memory access. Unfortunately, the number of registers is limited since only a few bits are reserved to select a register. Register addressing is a form of direct addressing, because we are interested in the number in the register, rather than using that number as a memory address. To assist in understanding Figure 6.2, some of the opcodes used by MIPS are shown in Figure 6.3. The values of rs, rd, rt should be the actual register numbers, and can fit in five bits since there are 32 registers.

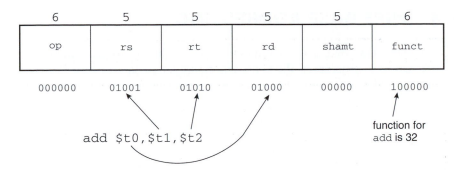

Figure 6.2 MIPS register addressing.

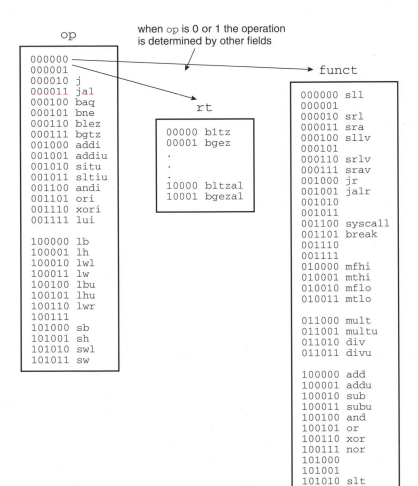

Figure 6.3 MIPS instruction opcodes.

6.4   MIPS BASE ADDRESSING

A data structure that is very important in computer programming is the record, called a structure in the C programming language. It is a collection of variables treated as a unit. For example, a personnel record might include name, address, age and department information. It is convenient to keep this information as a unit for each employee using a record or structure like:

```
struct personnel
  char name[80]
  char address[100]
  int age
  char department[10]
```

In base register addressing we add a small constant to a pointer held in a register. The register may point to a structure or some other collection of data, and we need to load a value at a constant offset from the beginning of the structure. Because each MIPS instruction fits in one word, the size of the constant is limited to 16 bits. The syntax is

```
lw rd,i(rb)
```

For example, if $t0 pointed to the base of a record or structure, we could get at the fields using

```
lw $t1,4($t0)
lw $t2,8($t0)
lw $t3,16($t0)
etc...
```

We have used a form of base addressing with zero offset (Figure 6.4) in `length.a` (line 21) (p. 52). As mentioned, this form of addressing is known

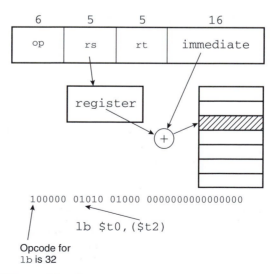

Figure 6.4   MIPS base addressing.

as indirect addressing since the operand is at the memory location whose address is in a register.

6.5   MIPS IMMEDIATE ADDRESSING

Immediate addressing (Figure 6.5) means that one operand is a constant within the instruction itself. Line 23 of `length.a` is an example of this addressing mode. Immediate addressing has the advantage of not requiring an extra memory access to fetch the operand, but the operand is limited to 16 bits in size.

The jump instruction format can also be considered an example of immediate addressing, since the destination is held in the instruction. Figure 6.6 illustrates this using line 25 of `length.a`.

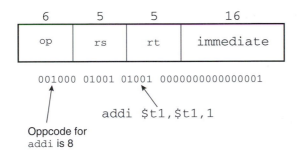

Figure 6.5   MIPS immediate addressing using `add`.

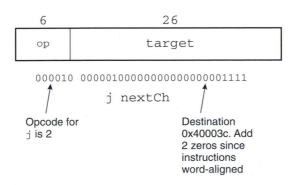

Figure 6.6   MIPS immediate addressing using `j`.

6.6 MIPS PC-RELATIVE ADDRESSING

PC-relative addressing (Figure 6.7), where the address is the sum of the program counter and a constant in the instruction, is used for conditional branches like line 22 of `length.a`. Branch instructions can only move 32 768 above or below the program counter because the offset is a 16-bit two's complement number (see Sections 2.5 and 2.6).

6.7 EXAMPLE PROGRAM USING BASE

ADDRESSING

Program `minmax.a` is another interesting program using the base addressing mode of Figure 6.4 with zero offset. It searches an array of words for the biggest and smallest elements. The

        .word

directive is used to set up an array of 15 four-byte words in the data section. An array data structure is a named list of items stored in memory, as shown in Figure 6.8.

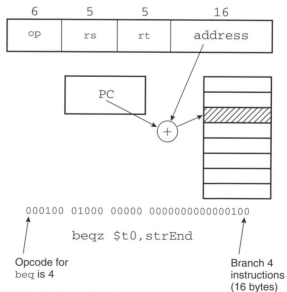

Figure 6.7 MIPS PC-relative addressing.

Memory

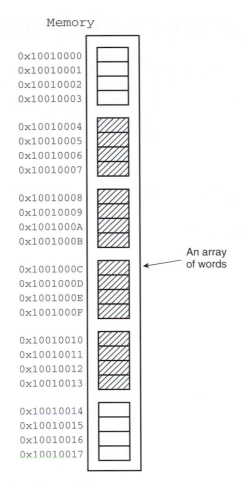

Figure 6.8 An array of words stored in memory.

Line 32 then uses the `lw` instruction to load each word into a register. An important difference between a pointer to a word and a pointer to a character is that the word pointer must be incremented by four each time round the loop (line 40), since each word occupies four memory locations.

```
1    ## minmax.a - print min, max of array elements.
2    ##
3    ## Assumes the array has at least two elements (a[0]
4    ## and a[1]). It initializes both min and max to a[0]
5    ## and then goes through the loop count-1 times.
6    ## This program will use pointers.
7    ##
8    ##        t0 - points to array elements in turn
```

```
 9    ##       t1 - contains count of elements
10    ##       t2 - contains min
11    ##       t3 - contains max
12    ##       t4 - each word from array in turn
13    ##
14
15    #################################################
16    #                    \                          #
17    #                text segment                   #
18    #                                               #
19    #################################################
20
21            .text
22            .globl __start
23    __start:
24            la $t0,array      # $t0 will point to elements
25            lw $t1,count      # exit loop when $t1 is 0
26            lw $t2,($t0)      # initialize both min ($t2)
27            lw $t3,($t0)      #       and max ($t3) to a[0]
28            add $t0,$t0,4     # pointer to start at a[1]
29            add $t1,$t1,-1    # and go round count-1 times
30
31
32    loop:   lw $t4,($t0)      # load next word from array
33            bge $t4,$t2,notMin
34                             # skip if a[i] >= min
35            move $t2,$t4      # copy a[i] to min
36    notMin: ble $t4,$t3,notMax
37                             # skip if a[i] <= max
38            move $t3,$t4      # copy a[i] to max
39    notMax: add $t1,$t1,-1    # decrement counter
40            add $t0,$t0,4     # increment pointer by word
41            bnez $t1,loop     # and continue if counter>0
42
43            la $a0,ans1
44            li $v0,4
45            syscall          # print "min = "
46
47            move $a0,$t2
48            li $v0,1
49            syscall          # print min
50
51            la $a0,ans2
52            li $v0,4
53            syscall          # print "\nmax = "
54
```

```
55              move $a0,$t3
56              li $v0,1
57              syscall          # print max
58
59              la $a0,endl       # system call to print
60              li $v0,4          # out a newline
61              syscall
62
63              li $v0,10
64              syscall          # au revoir...
65
66      ################################################
67      #                                              #
68      #              data segment                    #
69      #                                              #
70      ################################################
71
72              .data
73
74      array:    .word 3,4,2,6,12,7,18,26,2,14,19,7,8,12,13
75      count:    .word 15
76      endl:     .asciiz "\n"
77      ans1:     .asciiz "min = "
78      ans2:     .asciiz "\nmax = "
79
80      ##
81      ## end of file minmax.a
```

Two more example programs that test your understanding of arrays of words are loop1.a and loop6.a.

```
1       ## Start of file loop1.a
2       ##
3       ## Question:
4       ## calculate the sum of the elements in "array"
5       ## "count" holds the number of elements in "array"
6       ##
7       ## Output format must be:
8       ## "sum = 15"
9
10      ################################################
11      #                                              #
12      #              text segment                    #
13      #                                              #
14      ################################################
```

```
15
16              .text
17              .globl __start
18  __start:                    # execution starts here
19
20
21  # Any changes above this line will be discarded by
22  # mipsmark. Put your answer between dashed lines.
23  #------------ start cut --------------------------
24
25
26
27  #------------  end cut  --------------------------
28  # Any changes below this line will be discarded by
29  # mipsmark. Put your answer between dashed lines.
30
31  ###############################################
32  #                                             #
33  #              data segment                   #
34  #                                             #
35  ###############################################
36
37              .data
38  array:      .word 3,4,2,6
39  count:      .word 4
40  ans1:       .asciiz "sum = "
41  endl:       .asciiz "\n"
42  ##
43  ## End of file loop1.a


 1  ## Start of file loop6.a
 2  ##
 3  ## Question:
 4  ## "numbers" is an array of five words.
 5  ## Calculate the sum of all elements in "numbers"
 6  ## whose value is less than 1000.
 7  ##
 8  ## Output format must be:
 9  ## "sum = 11"
10
11  ###############################################
12  #                                             #
13  #              text segment                   #
14  #                                             #
15  ###############################################
```

```
16
17              .text
18              .globl __start
19   __start:                     # execution starts here
20
21
22   # Any changes above this line will be discarded by
23   # mipsmark. Put your answer between dashed lines.
24   #------------ start cut --------------------------
25
26
27
28   #------------  end cut  --------------------------
29   # Any changes below this line will be discarded by
30   # mipsmark. Put your answer between dashed lines.
31
32   #################################################
33   #                                               #
34   #               data segment                    #
35   #                                               #
36   #################################################
37
38              .data
39   numbers:
40              .word 3,2000,2,6,2000
41   ans:       .asciiz "sum = "
42   endl:      .asciiz "\n"
43   ##
44   ## End of file loop6.a
```

Further example programs that test your understanding of program loops using arrays of words are in Appendix A.3.

6.8   EXAMPLE PROGRAM USING INDEXED ADDRESSING

A useful mode for accessing elements of an array is called 'indexed addressing'. The assembler gives the programmer the option of using this mode with a pseudo-instruction, since this mode cannot fit into the instruction formats in Figure 6.1. The index of an element in an array is its position in the list, with zero usually referring to the first item. The idea is to use the contents of a register as an index, and add this index to the 'base address' specified in the instruction. The syntax is:

```
lw rd,addr(rx)
```

A good way to visualize indexed addressing is to think of the second operand as an array access like

```
addr[rx]
```

This mode also applies to other load and store instructions like lb. If the quantity to be added to the register does not fit in 16 bits, the assembler generates this addressing mode as a pseudo-instruction. Program count.a uses indexed addressing to go along a string counting the occurrences of a particular character.

```
 1     ## count.a - count the occurrences of a specific
 2     ## character in string "str".
 3     ## Indexed addressing used to access array elements.
 4     ##
 5     ##       t0 - holds each byte from string in turn
 6     ##       t1 - index into array
 7     ##       t2 - count of occurrences
 8     ##       t3 - holds the character to count
 9     ##
10
11     ################################################
12     #                                              #
13     #                 text segment                 #
14     #                                              #
15     ################################################
16
17             .text
18             .globl __start
19       __start:
20             li $t1,0        # $t1 will be the array index
21             li $t2,0        # $t2 will be the counter
22             lb $t3,char     # and $t3 will hold the char
23
24     loop:   lb $t0,str($t1) # fetch next char
25             beqz $t0,strEnd # if it's a null, exit loop
26             bne $t0,$t3,con # not null; same as char?
27             add $t2,$t2,1   # yes,increment counter
28     con:    add $t1,$t1,1   # increase index
29             j loop          # and continue
```

```
30
31     strEnd:
32             la $a0,ans       # system call to print
33             li $v0,4         # out a message
34             syscall
35
36             move $a0,$t2     # system call to print
37             li $v0,1         # out the count worked out
38             syscall
39
40             la $a0,endl      # system call to print
41             li $v0,4         # out a newline
42             syscall
43
44             li $v0,10
45             syscall          # au revoir...
46
47     ##################################################
48     #                                                #
49     #                 data segment                   #
50     #                                                #
51     ##################################################
52
53             .data
54     str:    .asciiz "abceebceebeebbacacb"
55     char:   .asciiz "e"
56     ans:    .asciiz "Count is "
57     endl:   .asciiz "\n"
58
59     ##
60     ## end of file count.a
```

Line 24 uses a register as an index into an array. Since str is a 32-bit address, this will not fit in any of the formats in Figure 6.1. The assembler uses $1 to build the address and then uses the base addressing mode, Figure 6.4, to access the operand.

```
        lb $t0,str($t1)
```

becomes (str has the value 0x10010000)

```
        lui $at,4097
        addu $at,$at,$t1
        lb $t0,($at)
```

6.9 BASE REGISTER ADDRESSING VS. INDEXED ADDRESSING

The indexed addressing and base register addressing modes are closely related. In indexed addressing, the base (for example the array start) is part of the instruction and the index is in the register, to allow us to increment the register each time through a loop or otherwise calculate the index.

In base register addressing, the base is in the register and the offset is part of the instruction, because members of high-level language structures are always at a fixed offset from the beginning of the structure. By putting the base in a register we can use the register as a pointer to the structure. To make this mode more useful, MIPS has the `la` instruction for loading a pointer (the address) into a register. In both cases the address used is the sum of the item before the brackets and the item inside them.

6.10 SUMMARY

The different ways of determining the address of an operand are called addressing modes. Every MIPS instruction consists of a single 32-bit word aligned on a word boundary. Instructions using register addressing execute quickly because they avoid the delays associated with memory access. In base register addressing a small constant is added to a pointer held in a register. Immediate addressing has the advantage of not requiring an extra memory access to fetch the operand, but the operand is limited to 16 bits in size. Indexed addressing uses the contents of a register as an index, and adds this index to the base address specified in the instruction.

EXERCISES

6.1   What is an addressing mode?

6.2   How many bytes are needed to store each MIPS instruction?

6.3   How many bits are needed to specify a MIPS register in an instruction?

6.4   How big can an immediate constant be if it fits in a single instruction?

6.5   Using Figure 6.3 and Figure 6.1, determine the machine code for `lui` `$t3,15`. Verify your answer using XSPIM.

6.6   Using Figure 6.3 and Figure 6.1 determine the machine code for `add` `$t4,$t3,$t3`. Verify your answer using XSPIM.

CHAPTER 7

Logical, shift and rotate instructions

7.1 INTRODUCTION

This chapter first looks at shift and rotate instructions. It then considers logical instructions, showing in an example program how these instructions can be used to convert a decimal number to an ASCII string in hexadecimal format. Logical, shift and rotate instructions are all used to manipulate the individual bits of a word.

7.2 SHIFT AND ROTATE INSTRUCTIONS

Shift and rotate instructions can change the positions of all the bits in a word in interesting ways. The bits in a word can be shifted either to the left or to the right. If shifted to the left, a zero is always shifted into the low-order bit. A logical shift right puts a zero into the high-order bit, but in an arithmetic shift right, the high-order bit is preserved, as illustrated in Figure 7.1. This is so that if the number was a negative two's complement number, the sign will not be altered by the arithmetic shift right instruction. Shift instructions can be used to multiply or divide by powers of two.

Rotates are similar to shifts except that the bit which falls off one end is moved into the opposite end of the word. Rotate left is shown in Figure 7.2.

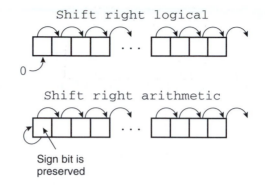

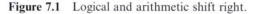

Figure 7.1 Logical and arithmetic shift right.

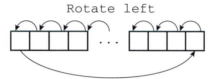

Figure 7.2 Rotate left instruction.

7.3 LOGICAL INSTRUCTIONS

There are five logical operations that have corresponding MIPS instructions – and, or, nor, not and xor. Nor means not or, and xor means exclusive or. The logical operations can be described using truth tables which are applied to the individual bits in a register or registers.

and, or, nor and xor require two operands; not requires only one.

not reverses the ones and zeros in a register, as shown in Figure 7.3.

The and instruction requires two operands. The result for each bit is one only if both operands are one (Figure 7.4). The format is like the add instruction – the second operand can be either a register or a constant. One of the commonest uses of the and instruction is to clear parts of a word, leaving the rest unchanged. This is achieved by putting a one in the positions that we want to keep, a zero in the positions we want to blank and using the and instruction (see Section 7.4).

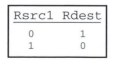

Figure 7.3 Truth table for not instruction.

Rsrc1	Src2	Rdest
0	0	0
0	1	0
1	0	0
1	1	1

Figure 7.4 Truth table for and instruction.

The or instruction also needs two operands. The result for each bit is one if either operand is a one (Figure 7.5). or can be used to set certain bits in a word, leaving other bits unchanged. This is achieved by putting a zero in the positions that we want to keep, a one in the positions we want to set and using the or instruction (see Section 7.4).

The xor instruction, exclusive or, is the same as or, except the result is zero if both operands are one (Figure 7.6). The nor instruction means not or (Figure 7.7). Table 7.1 lists the usage of some of the MIPS processor's logical instructions.

Rsrc1	Src2	Rdest
0	0	0
0	1	1
1	0	1
1	1	1

Figure 7.5 Truth table for or instruction.

Rsrc1	Src2	Rdest
0	0	0
0	1	1
1	0	1
1	1	0

Figure 7.6 Truth table for xor instruction.

Rsrc1	Src2	Rdest
0	0	1
0	1	0
1	0	0
1	1	0

Figure 7.7 Truth table for nor instruction.

Table 7.1 Examples of MIPS logical instructions.

Instruction	Example	
And	`and  $t1,$t2,$t3`	`#$t1 = $t2 & $t3`
And immediate	`andi $t1,$t2,8`	`#$t1 = $t2 & 8`
Or	`or   $t1,$t2,$t3`	`#$t1 = $t2	$t3`
Or immediate	`ori  $t1,$t2,15`	`#$t1 = $t2	15`
Xor	`xor  $t1,$t2,$t3`	`#$t1 = $t2 ⊕ $t3`
Xor immediate	`xori $t1,$t2,9`	`#$t1 = $t2 ① 9`
Nor	`nor  $t1,$t2,$t3`	`#$t1 = ~($t2 | $t3)`
Shift left logical	`all  $t1,$t2,3`	`#$t1 = $t2 << 3`
Shift left logical by variable	`sllv $t1,$t2,$t3`	`#$t1 = $t2 << $t3`
Shift right logical	`srl  $t1,$t2,10`	`#$t1 = $t2 >> 10`
Shift right logical by variable	`srlv $t1,$t2,$t3`	`#$t1 = $t2 >> $t3`
Shift right arithmetic	`sra  $t1,$t2,6`	`#$t1 = $t2 >> 6` `#sign extend`
Shift right arithmetic by variable	`srav $t1,$t2,$t3`	`#$t1 = $t2 >> $t3` `#sign extend`

7.4   AN EXAMPLE PROGRAM

The program hex.a asks a user for decimal number, converts it to hex, and prints the result.

```
 1    ##
 2    ## hex.a ask user for decimal number,
 3    ##   convert to hex, print the result.
 4    ##
 5    ##      t0 - count for 8 digits in word
 6    ##      t1 - each hex digit in turn
 7    ##      t2 - number read in
 8    ##      t3 - address of area used to set up
 9    ##           answer string
10    ##
11
12    ###############################################
13    #                                             #
14    #               text segment                  #
15    #                                             #
16    ###############################################
```

```
17
18              .text
19              .globl __start
20      __start:
21              la $a0,prompt     # print prompt on terminal
22              li $v0,4
23              syscall
24
25              li $v0,5          # syscall 5 reads an integer
26              syscall
27              move $t2,$v0      # $t2 holds hex number
28
29              la $a0,ans1       # print string before result
30              li $v0,4
31              syscall
32
33              li $t0,8          # eight hex digits in word
34              la $t3,result     # answer string set up here
35
36      loop:   rol $t2,$t2,4     # start with leftmost digit
37              and $t1,$t2,0xf   # mask one digit
38              ble $t1,9,print   # check if 0 to 9
39              add $t1,$t1,7     # 7 chars between '9' and 'A'
40      print:  add $t1,$t1,48    # ASCII '0' is 48
41              sb $t1,($t3)      # save in string
42              add $t3,$t3,1     # advance destination pointer
43              add $t0,$t0,-1    # decrement counter
44              bnez $t0,loop     # and continue if counter>0
45
46              la $a0,result     # print result on terminal
47              li $v0,4
48              syscall
49
50              li $v0,10
51              syscall           # au revoir...
52
53
54      ##################################################
55      #                                                #
56      #                data segment                    #
57      #                                                #
58      ##################################################
59
60              .data
61      result: .space 8
62              .asciiz "\n"
```

```
63    prompt: .asciiz "Enter decimal number: "
64    ans1:   .asciiz "Hexadecimal is "
65
66    ##
67    ## end of file hex.a
```

An interesting example use of the or instruction is to implement the la pseudo-instruction, which loads a 32-bit address into a register, for example line 21 of hex.a:

```
la $a0,prompt
```

The address of the prompt string is 0x1001000a. lui, load upper immediate, means load the immediate operand into the upper halfword of the register, setting the lower bits of the register are set to zero. The first component of the pseudo-instruction puts 0x1001 in the top 16 bits of the register using lui, then the logical or instruction is used to put the value 0x000a into the lower 16 bits, without altering the top 16:

```
lui $1,4097
ori $4,$1,10
```

Line 36 uses the rol instruction to bring each hexadecimal digit in turn into the least significant nibble of the register $t2 so that it can be converted to the corresponding ASCII code. It is important to study the layout of the ASCII table (Figure 2.8) to understand lines 38 to 40. The ASCII code for '0' is 48, and there are seven ASCII characters between '9' and 'A'.

One of the commonest uses of the and instruction is to clear parts of a word leaving the rest unchanged. An example of this is line 37, used to blank out everything in a word except the least significant nibble, to allow generation of the ASCII code for each hexadecimal digit in turn.

hex.a is also interesting because it uses the

```
.space n
```

assembler directive to allocate n bytes of space in the current segment (which must be the data segment in SPIM). Line 61 allocates eight bytes which are then used by the program to store the ASCII codes it wishes to print out (line 41), before making the system call to output a character string (line 48).

Another related program that illustrates the usage of the div and rem pseudo-instructions is dec.a, a program that converts a number to a decimal ASCII string:

```
1    ##
2    ##  dec.a ask user for decimal number,
3    ##  convert to ASCII string, print the result.
4    ##
5    ##      t0 - number read in, each quotient in turn
6    ##      t1 - points to memory for string
```

```
7    ##        t2 - each byte for the string in turn
8    ##
9
10   ##################################################
11   #                                                #
12   #                text segment                    #
13   #                                                #
14   ##################################################
15
16           .text
17           .globl __start
18   __start:
19           la $a0,prompt     # print prompt on terminal
20           li $v0,4
21           syscall
22
23           li $v0,5          # syscall 5 reads an integer
24           syscall
25           move $t0,$v0      # $t0 holds number
26
27           la $t1,result     # answer string set up here
28           add $t1,11
29
30           li $t2,0
31           sb $t2,($t1)      # save in string
32           sub $t1,1         # adjust destination pointer
33           li $t2,'\n'
34           sb $t2,($t1)      # save in string
35
36   loop:   rem $t2,$t0,10    # get the remainder
37           add $t2,48        # convert to ASCII code
38           sub $t1,1         # adjust destination pointer
39           sb $t2,($t1)      # save in string
40           div $t0,$t0,10    # get quotient
41           bnez $t0,loop     # and continue if quotient>0
42
43           la $a0,ans1       # print string before result
44           li $v0,4
45           syscall
46
47           move $a0,$t1      # print result on terminal
48           li $v0,4
49           syscall
50
51           li $v0,10
52           syscall           # au revoir...
```

```
53
54
55     ##################################################
56     #                                                #
57     #                 data segment                   #
58     #                                                #
59     ##################################################
60
61             .data
62     result: .space 12
63     ans1:   .asciiz "ASCII string is "
64     prompt: .asciiz "Enter decimal number: "
65
66     ##
67     ## end of file dec.a
```

It is not easy to convert a binary number to a decimal ASCII string because there is no direct correspondence between groups of bits and characters, as in hex.a. The correct procedure is to repeatedly divide the number by 10 (line 36), and use the remainder generated to construct the ASCII code (line 37). The step is repeated each time round the loop until the quotient produced equals zero (line 41).

This algorithm generates the characters in the reverse order needed, so the string is built from the end backwards (line 28). An alternative way to do this could be to use a rotate instruction to assemble the characters in the right order.

Two more example programs that test your understanding of the bit manipulation instructions are logic1.a and logic2.a.

```
1     ## Start of file logic1.a
2     ##
3     ## Question:
4     ## "numbers" is an array of five words.
5     ## Calculate the sum of all elements in "numbers"
6     ## that are not multiples of 4.
7     ## Use the and instruction, not div or rem for
8     ## this question.
9     ##
10    ## Output format must be:
11    ## "sum = 20"
12
13    ##################################################
14    #                                                #
15    #                 text segment                   #
16    #                                                #
17    ##################################################
```

```
18
19              .text
20              .globl __start
21      __start:                    # execution starts here
22
23
24      # Any changes above this line will be discarded by
25      # mipsmark. Put your answer between dashed lines.
26      #------------ start cut -------------------------
27
28
29
30      #------------  end cut  ------------------------
31      # Any changes below this line will be discarded by
32      # mipsmark. Put your answer between dashed lines.
33
34      ################################################
35      #                                              #
36      #              data segment                    #
37      #                                              #
38      ################################################
39
40              .data
41      numbers:
42              .word 3,4,12,28,17
43      ans:    .asciiz "sum = "
44      endl:   .asciiz "\n"
45      ##
46      ## End of file logic1.a



1       ## Start of file logic2.a
2       ##
3       ## Question:
4       ## "number" is a word.
5       ## Write it out in base 2 as a sequence of 32 bits.
6       ##
7       ## Output format must be:
8       ## "binary is = 00000000000000000000000000010001"
9
10      ################################################
11      #                                              #
12      #              text segment                    #
13      #                                              #
14      ################################################
```

```
15
16              .text
17              .globl __start
18      __start:                # execution starts here
19
20
21      # Any changes above this line will be discarded by
22      # mipsmark. Put your answer between dashed lines.
23      #------------ start cut -------------------------
24
25
26
27      #------------ end cut   -------------------------
28      # Any changes below this line will be discarded by
29      # mipsmark. Put your answer between dashed lines.
30
31      ###############################################
32      #                                             #
33      #               data segment                  #
34      #                                             #
35      ###############################################
36
37              .data
38      number: .word 17
39      result: .space 50
40      ans:    .asciiz "binary is = "
41      endl:   .asciiz "\n"
42      ##
43      ## End of file logic2.a
```

Further programs to test your understanding of logical, shift and rotate instructions are in Appendix A.4.

7.5   SUMMARY

Logical, shift and rotate instructions are all used to manipulate the individual bits of a word. The bits in a word can be shifted either to the left or to the right. Rotates are similar to shifts except the bit which falls off one end is put into the opposite end of the word. There are five logical operations that have corresponding MIPS instructions – and, or, nor, not and xor. nor means not or, and xor means exclusive or.

EXERCISES

7.1 Write down the truth table for the `xor` instruction.

7.2 What is the difference between logical and arithmetic shifts?

7.3 Describe an example use of the `and` instruction.

7.4 Describe how an assembler implements the `la` pseudo-instruction.

7.5 Give the algorithm to convert a number to a decimal ASCII string.

7.6 Give the algorithm to convert a number to a hexadecimal ASCII string.

CHAPTER 8

Stacks and procedures

8.1 INTRODUCTION

This chapter first introduces the stack data structure, and then illustrates its usage with a program to reverse a string using a stack. The techniques to support procedure calls in MIPS assembly language are then studied. Procedures allow programs to be broken into smaller more manageable units. They are fundamental to the development of programs longer than a few dozen statements. Procedures allow the reuse of the same group of statements many times by referring to them by name rather than repeating the code. In addition, procedures make large programs easier to read and understand. Stack frames, needed to implement procedure calls, are discussed. Two recursive programs are given that calculate Fibonacci's series and solve the Towers of Hanoi problem, and example code from a real compiler is discussed.

8.2 THE STACK

A stack of data elements is a last in, first out data structure. Items are added and removed from the top of the stack as shown in Figure 8.1. This is referred to as pushing and popping the stack. Because the stack is so frequently used, a special register, the stack pointer $sp, always holds the address of the top of the stack. The MIPS stack is upside down – elements are added at progressively lower memory addresses.

Pushing something on the stack is accomplished by two instructions.

```
sub $sp,$sp,4
sw $t0,($sp)
```

pushes the word in $t0 onto the stack. The sw instruction stores a word into memory from a register (Figure 8.2). The stack pointer is usually incremented

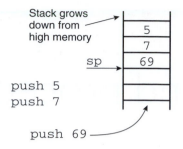

Stack grows
down from
high memory

sp

push 5
push 7

push 69

Figure 8.1   Stack data structure.

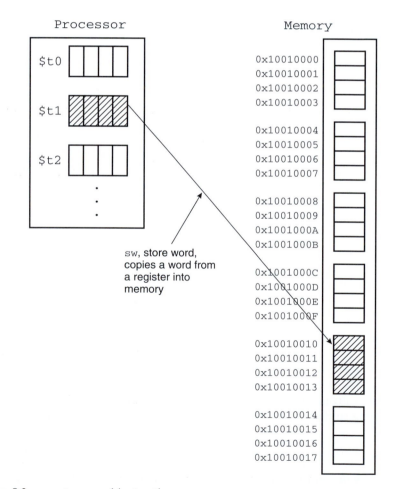

Processor

Memory

$t0

$t1

$t2

sw, store word,
copies a word from
a register into
memory

0x10010000
0x10010001
0x10010002
0x10010003

0x10010004
0x10010005
0x10010006
0x10010007

0x10010008
0x10010009
0x1001000A
0x1001000B

0x1001000C
0x1001000D
0x1001000E
0x1001000F

0x10010010
0x10010011
0x10010012
0x10010013

0x10010014
0x10010015
0x10010016
0x10010017

Figure 8.2   sw: store word instruction.

or decremented by four even if a byte is being pushed, so that $sp will always be aligned correctly if a word is subsequently pushed. The actions above are reversed to pop something off the stack.

```
lw $t0,($sp)
add $sp,$sp,4
```

pops the word from the top of stack into $t0. A stack can have many uses, for example to reverse the order of a list of data items or a string as shown in reverse.a.

```
1    ##
2    ## reverse.a - reverse the character
3    ## string "str".
4    ##
5    ##       t1 - points to the string
6    ##       t0 - holds each byte from string in turn
7    ##
8
9    ################################################
10   #                                              #
11   #                 text segment                 #
12   #                                              #
13   ################################################
14
15
16             .text
17             .globl __start
18   __start:                  # execution starts here
19             la $t1,str      # a0 points to the string
20   nextCh: lb $t0,($t1)      # get a byte from string
21             beqz $t0,strEnd # zero means end of string
22             sub $sp,$sp,4   # adjust stack pointer
23             sw $t0,($sp)    # PUSH the t0 register
24             add $t1,1       # move pointer one character
25             j nextCh        # go round the loop again
26
27   strEnd: la $t1,str        # a0 points to the string
28   store:  lb $t0,($t1)      # get a byte from string
29             beqz $t0,done   # zero means end of string
30             lw $t0,($sp)    # POP a value from the stack
31             add $sp,$sp,4   # and adjust the pointer
32             sb $t0,($t1)    # store in string
33             add $t1,1       # move pointer one character
```

```
34              j store
35
36   done:     la $a0,str       # system call to print
37             li $v0,4          # out a message
38             syscall
39
40             la $a0,endl       # system call to print
41             li $v0,4          # out a newline
42             syscall
43
44             li $v0,10
45             syscall           # au revoir...
46
47
48   ##################################################
49   #                                                #
50   #                data segment                    #
51   #                                                #
52   ##################################################
53
54             .data
55   str:      .asciiz "hello world"
56   endl:     .asciiz "\n"
57
58   ##
59   ## end of file reverse.a
```

Two example programs that test your understanding of the stack mechanism are stack1.a and stack6.a.

```
 1   ## Start of file stack1.a
 2   ##
 3   ## Question:
 4   ##
 5   ## Count the number of negative words on
 6   ## the stack by popping the stack until a
 7   ## non-negative word is found, and print
 8   ## out the number of words popped.
 9   ##
10   ## Do not rely on the existence on the "test"
11   ## or "num" variables, or the code above the
12   ## dashed line.
13   ##
```

```
14    ## Output format must be:
15    ## "Number is = 5"
16
17    ##################################################
18    #                                                #
19    #                 text segment                   #
20    #                                                #
21    ##################################################
22
23          .text
24          .globl __start
25    __start:                # execution starts here
26
27          la $t0,test       # This code sets up the stack
28          lw $t1,num        # Do not alter
29    loop: lw $t2,($t0)
30          sub $sp,$sp,4
31          sw $t2,($sp)
32          add $t0,$t0,4
33          add $t1,$t1,-1
34          bnez $t1,loop
35                            # Stack set up now....
36
37    # Any changes above this line will be discarded by
38    # mipsmark. Put your answer between dashed lines.
39    #----------- start cut -------------------------
40
41
42
43    #-----------  end cut  -------------------------
44    # Any changes below this line will be discarded by
45    # mipsmark. Put your answer between dashed lines.
46
47    ##################################################
48    #                                                #
49    #                 data segment                   #
50    #                                                #
51    ##################################################
52
53          .data
54    test: .word 2,0xffffffd5,0xfffabfff,-3,-4,-9
55    num:  .word 6
56    ans:  .asciiz "Number is = "
57    endl: .asciiz "\n"
58    ##
59    ## End of file stack1.a
```

```
 1    ## Start of file stack6.a
 2    ##
 3    ## Question:
 4    ##
 5    ## Count the number of words on
 6    ## the stack with at most four bits set
 7    ## by popping the stack until a
 8    ## word is found with five or more bits set,
 9    ## and print
10    ## out the number of words popped.
11    ##
12    ## Do not rely on the existence on the "test"
13    ## or "num" variables, or the code above the
14    ## dashed line.
15    ##
16    ## Output format must be:
17    ## "Number is = 4"
18
19    ################################################
20    #                                              #
21    #                text segment                  #
22    #                                              #
23    ################################################
24
25            .text
26            .globl __start
27    __start:                # execution starts here
28
29            la $t0,test      # This code sets up the stack
30            lw $t1,num       # Do not alter
31    loop:   lw $t2,($t0)
32            sub $sp,$sp,4
33            sw $t2,($sp)
34            add $t0,$t0,4
35            add $t1,$t1,-1
36            bnez $t1,loop
37                             # Stack set up now....
38
39    # Any changes above this line will be discarded by
40    # mipsmark. Put your answer between dashed lines.
41    #----------- start cut ------------------------
42
43
44
45    #----------- end cut  ------------------------
46    # Any changes below this line will be discarded by
```

```
47    # mipsmark. Put your answer between dashed lines.
48
49    ##################################################
50    #                                                #
51    #                  data segment                  #
52    #                                                #
53    ##################################################
54
55            .data
56    test:    .word 2,0xff,4,1,1,1
57    num:     .word 6
58    ans:     .asciiz "Number is = "
59    endl:    .asciiz "\n"
60    ##
61    ## End of file stack6.a
```

Further example programs that test your understanding of the stack instructions are in Appendix A.5.

8.3   PROCEDURE CALLS

A very important type of control structure is the code used to implement procedure and function calls. Procedures are the most important technique for structuring programs. We need a way to keep track of the calling location, so that the program can resume where it left off when the procedure finishes, and a way to pass parameters and return results. Also, a convention for creating local variables must be adopted.

The call/return mechanism in MIPS is very easy. The jump and link instruction puts the return address into a special register $ra before executing the code for the procedure, as shown in Figure 8.3.

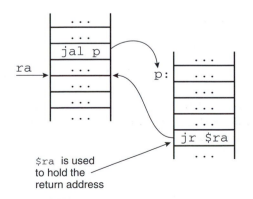

Figure 8.3   Procedure call mechanism.

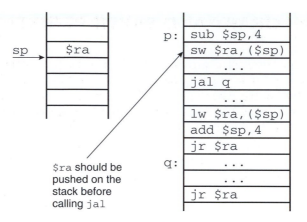

Figure 8.4 Using the stack for a return address.

At runtime, the processor puts the value PC+4 in `$ra` when `jal` is executed, and after the called procedure is finished it just has to do a jump register to return. If `p` calls another procedure, though, things are a bit more complicated – `p` has to save its return address on a stack, as shown in Figure 8.4, because the return address will be overwritten.

8.4   PASSING PARAMETERS

The first four parameters of a procedure are passed in the argument registers `$a0..$a3`. Additional parameters are passed on the stack. `$v0` and `$v1` are for returned values.

Thus, a procedure to see if a letter is a vowel would look like this:

```
vowelp: li $v0,0
        beq  $a0,'a',yes
        beq  $a0,'e',yes
        beq  $a0,'i',yes
        beq  $a0,'o',yes
        beq  $a0,'u',yes
        jr $ra
yes:    li $v0,1
        jr $ra
```

The procedure `vowelp` takes a single character as a parameter and returns one if the character is a (lower-case) vowel, otherwise it returns zero. It adopts the MIPS conventions for register usage.

8.5   TEMPORARY AND SAVED REGISTERS

When a procedure uses local variables, it is best to keep as many as possible in registers, because it is much faster to access registers than memory. The problem with this is that when one procedure calls another, the registers may have to be saved so that the values contained in them will not be lost.

There are two basic strategies for saving registers at a procedure call. 'Caller saves' means that the code that makes the call will put register values on the stack. 'Callee saves' means that the called procedure will do the saving. The advantage of caller saves is that the caller knows which registers it will be using, so it won't save a value not needed when it returns. The advantage of callee saves is that the callee knows which registers it needs and will only save these registers.

For example, if a procedure is using a variable that will not be needed after calling another procedure, it will keep it in a caller save register and not save the register. Thus by wisely selecting which values are stored in caller saved and which in callee saved, the number of loads and stores can be minimized.

In MIPS, the designers adopted the following conventions: $s0..$s7 are callee saves, which means that the caller can count on them being restored when control returns. $t0..$t9 are caller saves which, as the name implies, are usually temporary registers. If their values will be needed, the caller saves them before making the call. The called procedure can therefore modify any of the registers $t0..$t9 without constraint. For example:

```
code using $s0..$s7
jal p
$s0..$s7 have not changed,
    but $t0..$t9 may have been altered
```

There are two problems with using registers for local variables:

- What if there are not enough registers?
- What if the procedure wants to call another procedure?

Stack frames are used to solve these problems.

8.6   STACK FRAMES

In almost every modern programming language, a procedure may have local variables that are created on entry. Since a procedure returns only after all the procedures it has called have returned, procedure calls are said to behave in last in, first out (LIFO) fashion. If local variables are created on procedure entry and destroyed on procedure exit, a stack is the ideal data structure to hold them.

So far the simple stack data structure supports two operations – push and pop. However, local variables may be pushed in large batches on entry to procedures and popped in large batches on exit. Local variables are not always initialized as soon as they are created, and when many variables have been created we want to access those deep within the stack, so the simple push and pop model is no longer sufficient.

A special type of data structure that uses base register addressing, called the stack frame (Figure 8.5), is used to overcome these difficulties. Stack frames are used in procedure calls. The stack usually only grows on entry to a procedure. The compiler figures out how big the frame needs to be (for example, *n* bytes). The first thing it does in the body of the procedure is subtract *n* from the stack pointer, which allocates a structure of size *n* on the stack. This process is called the procedure prologue. The compiler shrinks the stack by the same amount *n* just before exiting from a procedure in the procedure epilogue. Sometimes a compiler finds it convenient to use a register which points to a fixed location within the stack frame, called a frame pointer, and access the local variables which reference it rather than the stack pointer itself. The stack pointer can then be used by the compiler to evaluate expressions.

Whenever it is necessary to access a local variable or parameter on the stack frame, base mode addressing using $fp as the base address is used, for example:

```
lw $s0,0($fp)
lw $s1,4($fp)
lw $s2,8($fp)
lw $s3,12($fp)
```

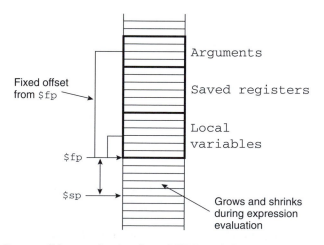

Figure 8.5 One possible organization for a MIPS stack frame.

Processors like the MIPS were designed for high-level language compilation, and as such are targeted at compilers rather than human programmers. When compiling a program the compiler simulates the runtime stack to help decide what values are placed in registers and what values are on the stack during procedure call. This is the motivation for the caller and callee save registers. Traffic between the processor and the memory is minimized at the expense of increasing the complexity in the compiler.

vowel.a prints out the number of vowels in the string str.

```
1     ##
2     ## vowel.a - prints out number of vowels in
3     ##            - the string str
4     ##
5     ##       a0 - points to the string
6     ##
7
8     ################################################
9     #                                              #
10    #                text segment                  #
11    #                                              #
12    ################################################
13
14            .text
15            .globl __start
16    __start:                 # execution starts here
17
18
19            la $a0,str
20            jal vcount       # call vcount
21
22            move $a0,$v0
23            li $v0,1
24            syscall          # print answer
25
26
27            la $a0,endl
28            li $v0,4
29            syscall          # print newline
30
31            li $v0,10
32            syscall          # au revoir...
33
```

```
34      #------------------------------------------------
35      # vowelp - takes a single character as a
36      # parameter and returns 1 if the character
37      # is a (lower case) vowel otherwise return 0.
38      #       a0 - holds character
39      #       v0 - returns 0 or 1
40      #------------------------------------------------
41
42      vowelp: li $v0,0
43              beq  $a0,'a',yes
44              beq  $a0,'e',yes
45              beq  $a0,'i',yes
46              beq  $a0,'o',yes
47              beq  $a0,'u',yes
48              jr $ra
49      yes:    li $v0,1
50              jr $ra
51
52
53      #------------------------------------------------
54      # vcount - use vowelp to count the vowels in a
55      # string.
56      #       a0 - holds string address
57      #       s0 - holds number of vowels
58      #       v0 - returns number of vowels
59      #------------------------------------------------
60
61      vcount:
62              sub $sp,$sp,16  # save registers on stack
63              sw $a0,0($sp)
64              sw $s0,4($sp)
65              sw $s1,8($sp)
66              sw $ra,12($sp)
67
68              li $s0,0        # count of vowels
69              move $s1,$a0    # address of string
70
71      nextc:  lb $a0,($s1)    # get each character
72              beqz $a0,done   # zero marks end
73              jal vowelp      # call vowelp
74              add $s0,$s0,$v0 # add 0 or 1 to count
75              add $s1,$s1,1   # move along string
76              b nextc
77      done:   move $v0,$s0    # use $v0 for result
78
79              lw $a0,0($sp)   # restore registers
```

```
80              lw $s0,4($sp)
81              lw $s1,8($sp)
82              lw $ra,12($sp)
83              add $sp,$sp,16
84              jr $ra
85
86
87     ##################################################
88     #                                                #
89     #                data segment                    #
90     #                                                #
91     ##################################################
92
93
94              .data
95     str:     .asciiz "long time ago in a galaxy far away"
96     endl:    .asciiz "\n"
97
98     ##
99     ## end of file vowel.a
```

We have already looked at the simple procedure vowelp. The vcount procedure repeatedly calls vowelp to count the vowels in a string. Because vcount calls another procedure it must save its return address on the stack, as the value in $ra will be overwritten (line 66). vcount uses $s0 and $s1 for quantities of interest because it calls another procedure that could change $t0 and $t1.

Two example programs that test your understanding of the procedure call mechanism are funct1.a and funct2.a.

```
1      ## Start of file funct1.a
2      ##
3      ## Question:
4      ## Write a function "addone" that takes an ascii
5      ## character in $a0.
6      ## If the character is a digit, increment it by
7      ## one. '9' should go to '0'.
8      ## If it is not a digit, return it unaltered
9      ## in $v0.
10     ##
11     ## Write a function "stradd" that goes along
12     ## a string $a0 calling "addone" to add one
13     ## to all the digits in the string and stores
14     ## the returned characters into the string.
15     ##
```

```
16    ## Output format must be:
17    ## "abc1067xyz"
18
19    #################################################
20    #                                               #
21    #                 text segment                  #
22    #                                               #
23    #################################################
24
25            .text
26            .globl __start
27    __start:                    # execution starts here
28
29
30            li $a0,'5'       # test addone function
31            jal addone
32            bne $v0,'6',exit
33
34            la $a0,str
35            jal stradd        # call stradd function
36            li $v0,4
37            syscall
38
39    exit:   li $v0,10
40            syscall           # au revoir...
41
42    # Any changes above this line will be discarded by
43    # mipsmark. Put your answer between dashed lines.
44    #------------ start cut --------------------------
45
46
47
48    #------------  end cut   -------------------------
49    # Any changes below this line will be discarded by
50    # mipsmark. Put your answer between dashed lines.
51
52    #################################################
53    #                                               #
54    #                 data segment                  #
55    #                                               #
56    #################################################
57
58            .data
59    str:    .asciiz "abc0956xyz\n"
60    ##
61    ## End of file funct1.a
```

```
 1    ## Start of file funct2.a
 2    ##
 3    ## Question:
 4    ## Write a function "hexint" that takes the address
 5    ## of an ascii character string in $a0.
 6    ## The string will represent a number in
 7    ## hexadecimal and will only contain '0' to '9'
 8    ## and 'A' to 'F'.
 9    ## Return the actual number in the register $v0.
10    ## Remember that the most significant nibble
11    ## will be first in the string.
12    ##
13    ## Output format must be:
14    ## "Number is = 1960"
15
16    #################################################
17    #                                               #
18    #               text segment                    #
19    #                                               #
20    #################################################
21
22            .text
23            .globl __start
24    __start:                  # execution starts here
25
26
27            la $a0,ans
28            li $v0,4
29            syscall
30
31            la $a0,str
32            jal hexint        # call hexint function
33
34            move $a0,$v0
35            li $v0,1
36            syscall
37
38            la $a0,endl       # system call to print
39            li $v0,4          # out a newline
40            syscall
41
42    exit:   li $v0,10
43            syscall           # au revoir...
44
45    # Any changes above this line will be discarded by
46    # mipsmark. Put your answer between dashed lines.
```

```
47    #------------ start cut -------------------------
48
49
50
51    #------------ end cut   -------------------------
52    # Any changes below this line will be discarded by
53    # mipsmark. Put your answer between dashed lines.
54
55    ################################################
56    #                                              #
57    #              data segment                    #
58    #                                              #
59    ################################################
60
61            .data
62    str:    .asciiz "7A8"
63    ans:    .asciiz "Number is = "
64    endl:   .asciiz "\n"
65    ##
66    ## End of file funct2.a
```

8.7   ASSEMBLY CODE FROM A REAL

COMPILER

This section shows the assembly code and stack frame that might be used by a compiler to implement the following fragment of high-level language code:

```
int fun1(int n, int p)
{
        int i,j;
        i = 7;
        j = 9;
        if (n == 1)
                p = i;
        else
                p = j;
        return p;
}

int fun2(int num)
```

```
{
        int q,r;
        q = 5;
        r = fun1(q, num);
        return r;
}

int fun3(int y, int x)
{
        int a,b;
        a = fun1(5, 7);
        b = fun2(8);
        return a + b;
}
```

This code does not do anything useful; the three functions simply contain a number of arguments and local variables to illustrate the compiler's use of a stack frame. The assembly code produced is obviously inefficient, but if the compiler was asked to optimize the code, unnecessary space would not be wasted on the stack frames for these simple functions.

```
1     fun1:    subu     $sp,$sp,16
2              sw       $fp,8($sp)
3              move     $fp,$sp
4              sw       $4,16($fp)
5              sw       $5,20($fp)
6              li       $2,0x00000007
7              sw       $2,0($fp)
8              li       $2,0x00000009
9              sw       $2,4($fp)
10             lw       $2,16($fp)
11             li       $3,0x00000001
12             bne      $2,$3,$L2
13             lw       $2,0($fp)
14             sw       $2,20($fp)
15             j        $L3
16    $L2:     lw       $2,4($fp)
17             sw       $2,20($fp)
18    $L3:     lw       $2,20($fp)
19             j        $L1
20    $L1:     move     $sp,$fp
21             lw       $fp,8($sp)
22             addu     $sp,$sp,16
23             j        $31
24
25
```

```
26    fun2:    subu     $sp,$sp,24
27             sw       $31,20($sp)
28             sw       $fp,16($sp)
29             move     $fp,$sp
30             sw       $4,24($fp)
31             li       $2,0x00000005
32             sw       $2,8($fp)
33             lw       $4,8($fp)
34             lw       $5,24($fp)
35             jal      fun1
36             sw       $2,12($fp)
37             lw       $2,12($fp)
38             j        $L4
39    $L4:     move     $sp,$fp
40             lw       $31,20($sp)
41             lw       $fp,16($sp)
42             addu     $sp,$sp,24
43             j        $31
44
45    fun3:    subu     $sp,$sp,24
46             sw       $31,20($sp)
47             sw       $fp,16($sp)
48             move     $fp,$sp
49             sw       $4,24($fp)
50             sw       $5,28($fp)
51             li       $4,0x00000005
52             li       $5,0x00000007
53             jal      fun1
54             sw       $2,8($fp)
55             li       $4,0x00000008
56             jal      fun2
57             sw       $2,12($fp)
58             lw       $2,8($fp)
59             lw       $4,12($fp)
60             addu     $3,$2,$4
61             move     $2,$3
62             j        $L5
63    $L5:     move     $sp,$fp
64             lw       $31,20($sp)
65             lw       $fp,16($sp)
66             addu     $sp,$sp,24
67             j        $31
```

Space is allocated on the stack frame for the arguments to fun1 (Figure 8.6) and fun2 (Figure 8.7). Figure 8.8 shows the stack frame for fun3.

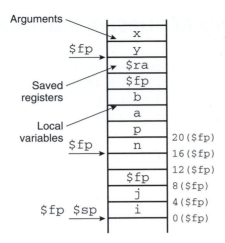

Figure 8.6 Stack frame for fun1.

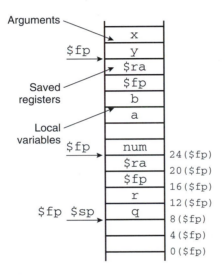

Figure 8.7 Stack frame for fun2.

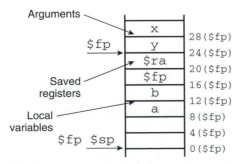

Figure 8.8 Stack frame for fun3.

8.8 EXAMPLE RECURSIVE PROGRAMS

Recursion is an important feature of many programming languages. A recursive task is one that calls itself. With each invocation, the problem is reduced to a smaller problem (reducing case) until the task arrives at some terminal or base case which stops the process.

8.8.1 FIBONACCI'S RABBITS

The original problem that Fibonacci investigated, in the year 1202, was how fast rabbits could breed in ideal circumstances. Suppose a newly born pair of rabbits, one male and one female, are put in a field. Rabbits are sexually mature after one month so that at the end of its second month a female can produce another pair of rabbits. Suppose that our rabbits never die and that females always produces one new pair (one male, one female) every month from the second month on. How many pairs will there be in one year?

- At the end of the first month they mate, but there is still one only one pair.
- At the end of the second month the female produces a new pair, so now there are two pairs of rabbits in the field.
- At the end of the third month, the original female produces a second pair, making three pairs in all in the field.
- At the end of the fourth month, the original female has produced yet another new pair, and the female born two months ago produces her first pair also, making five pairs.

Fibonacci's series therefore looks like:

$$
\begin{array}{lccccccccccc}
n & 0 & 1 & 2 & 3 & 4 & 5 & 6 & 7 & 8 & 9 \cdots \\
fib(n) & 0 & 1 & 1 & 2 & 3 & 5 & 8 & 13 & 21 & 34 \cdots
\end{array}
$$

One way to write a program to work these numbers out is to use a loop starting from the base case, as shown in the file `fibloop.a`.

```
 1   ##
 2   ## fibloop.a - looping implementation of the
 3   ##              Fibonacci function.
 4   ##
 5   ##      a0 - value to test function
 6   ##
 7
 8   ################################################
 9   #                                              #
10   #                text segment                  #
11   #                                              #
12   ################################################
```

```
13
14              .text
15              .globl __start
16     __start:                 # execution starts here
17              li $a0,9
18              jal fib          # call fib
19              move $a0,$v0      # print result
20              li $v0, 1
21              syscall
22
23              la $a0,endl
24              li $v0,4
25              syscall
26
27              li $v0,10
28              syscall          # au revoir...
29
30     #-----------------------------------------------
31     # fib - looping implementation of the
32     # Fibonacci function.
33     #       a0 - holds parameter n
34     #       t0 - save second last element computed
35     #       t1 - used to work out each new element
36     #       v0 - returns result
37     #-----------------------------------------------
38
39     fib:    move $v0,$a0     # initialize last element
40             blt $a0,2,done  # fib(0)=0, fib(1)=1
41
42             li $t0,0         # second last element
43             li $v0,1         # last element
44
45     loop:   add $t1,$t0,$v0 # get next value
46             move $t0,$v0     # update second last
47             move $v0,$t1     # update last element
48             sub $a0,1        # decrement count
49             bgt $a0,1,loop  # exit loop when count=1
50     done:   jr $ra
51
52     ##################################################
53     #                                                #
54     #              data segment                      #
55     #                                                #
56     ##################################################
57
58              .data
```

```
59    endl:    .asciiz "\n"
60
61    ##
62    ## end of file fibloop.a
```

In order to increase our understanding of procedures and stack frames, let us look at a recursive implementation. This implementation will be less efficient at runtime due to all the instructions needed to maintain the stack frames, and since there is a limited amount of memory available for a stack, if the function is called with a large parameter, space for the stack may run out.

We note that

$$fib(n) = fib(n-2) + fib(n-1)$$

and that

$$fib(0) = 0 \quad fib(1) = 1$$

The steps to evaluate $fib(n)$ recursively are shown in Figure 8.9.

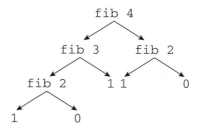

Figure 8.9 Recursive implementation of Fibonacci function.

```
1     ##
2     ## fib.a - recursive implementation of the
3     ##          Fibonacci function.
4     ##
5     ##      a0 - value to test function
6     ##
7
8     ###################################################
9     #                                                 #
10    #                 text segment                    #
11    #                                                 #
12    ###################################################
```

```
13
14          .text
15          .globl __start
16  __start:                  # execution starts here
17          li $a0,9
18          jal fib            # call fib
19          move $a0,$v0       # print result
20          li $v0, 1
21          syscall
22
23          la $a0,endl
24          li $v0,4
25          syscall
26
27          li $v0,10
28          syscall            # au revoir...
29
30  #----------------------------------------------
31  # fib - recursive implementation of the
32  # Fibonacci function.
33  #       a0 - holds parameter n
34  #       s0 - holds fib(n-1)
35  #       v0 - returns result
36  #----------------------------------------------
37
38  fib:    sub $sp,$sp,12  # save registers on stack
39          sw $a0,0($sp)
40          sw $s0,4($sp)
41          sw $ra,8($sp)
42
43          bgt $a0,1,notOne
44          move $v0,$a0    # fib(0)=0, fib(1)=1
45          b fret          # if n<=1
46
47  notOne: sub $a0,$a0,1   # param = n-1
48          jal fib         # compute fib(n-1)
49          move $s0,$v0    # save fib(n-1)
50
51          sub $a0,$a0,1   # set param to n-2
52          jal fib         # and make recursive call
53          add $v0,$v0,$s0 # add fib(n-2)
54
55  fret:   lw $a0,0($sp)   # restore registers
56          lw $s0,4($sp)
57          lw $ra,8($sp)
58          add $sp,$sp,12
```

```
59              jr $ra
60
61      ##################################################
62      #                                                #
63      #                data segment                    #
64      #                                                #
65      ##################################################
66
67              .data
68      endl:   .asciiz "\n"
69
70      ##
71      ## end of file fib.a
```

Note that a programming language that does not permit recursive procedures, for example older versions of Fortran, need not allocate frames on a stack, but can use ordinary memory for the local variables, since only one invocation of a procedure may be active at a time.

An example program that will test your understanding of the the recursion concept is recur1.a.

```
 1      ## Start of file recur1.a
 2      ##
 3      ## Question:
 4      ##
 5      ## Write a function named search that will do a
 6      ## depth first search of a tree for a marked
 7      ## node. A marked node is one that has a value
 8      ## field equal to 1. Only one node in the tree is
 9      ## marked.
10      ##
11      ## The parameters to search are a pointer to the
12      ## tree and the current depth. On each recursive
13      ## call add 1 to the depth. This parameter is
14      ## used to keep track of the path from the root
15      ## to the marked node; as you visit a node, you
16      ## will call a procedure named store_path to
17      ## record the fact that you have visited this
18      ## node. The code for store_path and print_path
19      ## (called after you get back from the procedure)
20      ## have been written for you -- all you need to
21      ## do is understand how to set up their parameters
22      ## and make the call.
23      ##
```

```
24     ## The code for search could look like:
25     ##            call store_path
26     ##            if (value == 1)
27     ##              return 1
28     ##            if (left tree exists)
29     ##               if (search(left tree, depth+1))
30     ##                 return 1
31     ##            if (right tree exists)
32     ##               return search(right tree, depth+1)
33     ##            return 0
34     ##
35     ## Output format must be:
36     ## "apple-->orange-->plum-->grape-->star-->passion"
37
38     #################################################
39     #                                               #
40     #              text segment                     #
41     #                                               #
42     #################################################
43
44             .text
45             .globl __start
46     __start:                    # execution starts here
47
48             la $a0,tree
49             li $a1,0
50             jal search         # search the tree
51
52             jal print_path     # print the path
53                                # to the node with val=1
54             li $v0,10
55             syscall            # au revoir....
56
57
58     #------------------------------------------------
59     # store_path - store pointer at level n in the path
60     #       a0 - holds pointer to string
61     #       a1 - level to use in path
62     #------------------------------------------------
63     store_path:
64             mul $t0,$a1,4    # each pointer is 4 bytes
65             sw $a0,path($t0)# save pointer to the name
66             addi $t0,$t0,4   # make the next entry
67             sw $0,path($t0)  #  equal to 0.
68             jr $ra
69
```

```
70
71       #-----------------------------------------------
72       # print_path() - print the items stored in path
73       #-----------------------------------------------
74       print_path:
75               li $t0,0          # i
76               mul $t1,$t0,4     # each pointer is 4 bytes
77               lw $a0,path($t1)
78       next:   li $v0,4
79               syscall           # print path[i]
80               addi $t0,$t0,1    # i++
81               mul $t1,$t0,4     # each pointer is 4 bytes
82               lw $a0,path($t1)
83               beqz $a0,done
84               move $t1,$a0
85               la $a0,arrow
86               li $v0,4
87               syscall           # print "-->"
88               move $a0,$t1
89               b next
90       done:   la $a0,endl
91               li $v0,4
92               syscall           # print newline
93               jr $ra
94
95       # Any changes above this line will be discarded by
96       # mipsmark. Put your answer between dashed lines.
97       #----------- start cut ------------------------
98
99
100
101      #-----------  end cut  ------------------------
102      # Any changes below this line will be discarded by
103      # mipsmark. Put your answer between dashed lines.
104
105      ################################################
106      #                                              #
107      #             data segment                     #
108      #                                              #
109      ################################################
110
111              .data
112
113      # The binary tree.  Note that each node has four
114      # words - a pointer to the name, pointers to
115      # left and right subtrees, and the integer
```

```
116    # value field.
117
118    path:    .space 40
119
120    tree:    .word name0, node1, node2, 0
121    node1:   .word name1, node3, node4, 0
122    node2:   .word name2, node5, node6, 0
123    node3:   .word name3, node7, 0, 0
124    node4:   .word name4, node8, node9, 0
125    node5:   .word name5, 0, 0, 0
126    node6:   .word name6, node10, node11, 0
127    node7:   .word name7, 0, 0, 0
128    node8:   .word name8, 0, 0, 0
129    node9:   .word name9, node12, node13, 0
130    node10:  .word name10, 0, 0, 0
131    node11:  .word name11, 0, 0, 0
132    node12:  .word name12, node14, node15, 0
133    node13:  .word name13, 0, 0, 0
134    node14:  .word name14, 0, 0, 1
135    node15:  .word name15, node16, node17, 0
136    node16:  .word name16, 0, 0, 0
137    node17:  .word name17, 0, 0, 0
138
139    name0:   .asciiz "apple"
140    name1:   .asciiz "orange"
141    name2:   .asciiz "banana"
142    name3:   .asciiz "pear"
143    name4:   .asciiz "plum"
144    name5:   .asciiz "peach"
145    name6:   .asciiz "nectarine"
146    name7:   .asciiz "pineapple"
147    name8:   .asciiz "grapefruit"
148    name9:   .asciiz "grape"
149    name10:  .asciiz "melon"
150    name11:  .asciiz "avocado"
151    name12:  .asciiz "star"
152    name13:  .asciiz "mango"
153    name14:  .asciiz "passion"
154    name15:  .asciiz "cantaloupe"
155    name16:  .asciiz "watermelon"
156    name17:  .asciiz "apricot"
157
158    endl:    .asciiz "\n"
159    arrow:   .asciiz "-->;"
160    ##
161    ## End of file recur1.a
```

8.8.2 THE TOWERS OF HANOI

The above program to work out the numbers in the Fibonacci series is interesting because it tests that the procedure uses the stack frame correctly. It would, however, be much more efficient to start at the base case and use a simple loop to work out the numbers, saving all the loads and stores involved in setting up a stack frame. There are some programs, however, which would be very difficult to write without the use of recursion. An example is the Towers of Hanoi problem.

Legend has it that a group of Eastern monks are the keepers of three towers on which sit 64 golden rings. Originally all 64 rings were stacked on one tower with each ring smaller than the one beneath. The monks are to move the rings from this first tower to the third tower one at a time but never moving a larger ring on top of a smaller one. Once the 64 rings have all been moved, the world will come to an end.

Despite the seemingly convoluted nature of this puzzle, there is a simple recursive solution. If we need to move n rings from a tower (call it start) to another tower (called end) using the remaining tower as a spare, we can recursively move the top $n-1$ from start to spare using end as the spare (Figure 8.10). Notice that in the recursive solution for $n-1$ rings, we exchange the roles of the spare and end towers. Now we can move the bottom ring from start to end (Figure 8.11). Finally, we do another recursive move of the $n-1$ we put onto spare to the end tower, using start as the spare (Figure 8.11).

Program `hanoi.a` is a MIPS assembly language program to solve the Towers of Hanoi.

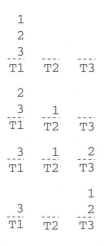

Figure 8.10 Recursively move the top $n-1$ rings from the start tower to the spare tower using the end tower as the spare tower.

```
                         1
        ----    --3    --2
        T1      T2     T3

        --1     --3    --2
        T1      T2     T3

                 2
        --1     --3    ----
        T1      T2     T3

                 1
                 2
        ----    --3    ----
        T1      T2     T3
```

Figure 8.11 Recursively move $n-1$ rings from the spare tower to the end tower using the start tower as the spare tower.

```
 1    ##
 2    ## hanoi.a - recursive implementation of the
 3    ##            towers of hanoi
 4    ##
 5    ##
 6
 7    ##################################################
 8    #                                                #
 9    #                text segment                    #
10    #                                                #
11    ##################################################
12
13            .text
14            .globl __start
15    __start:
16
17            la $a0,tower1    # source
18            la $a1,tower2    # destination
19            la $a2,tower3    # temporary
20            lw $a3,numRings
21
22            jal moveStack    # call procedure
23
24            jal PrintTowers # Print answer
25
```

```
26              li $v0,10
27              syscall          # au revoir...
28
29
30      #-------------------------------------------------
31      # moveStack - recursive implementation of the
32      # towers of hanoi
33      #        a0 - source tower
34      #        a1 - destination tower
35      #        a2 - spare tower
36      #        a3 - number of rings
37      #        s0 - source tower
38      #        s1 - destination tower
39      #        s2 - spare tower
40      #-------------------------------------------------
41      moveStack:
42              sub $sp,$sp,32   # save registers on stack
43              sw $a0,0($sp)
44              sw $a1,4($sp)
45              sw $a2,8($sp)
46              sw $a3,12($sp)
47              sw $s0,16($sp)
48              sw $s1,20($sp)
49              sw $s2,24($sp)
50              sw $ra,28($sp)
51
52              beq $a3,1,moveOne
53                               # Move one ring only
54
55              move $s0,$a0    # keep copy of source tower
56              move $s1,$a1    # keep copy of destination
57              move $s2,$a2    # keep copy of spare tower
58
59              move $a0,$s0    # step 1:
60              move $a1,$s2    # destination = spare tower
61              move $a2,$s1
62              sub $a3,$a3,1   # move n-1 rings
63              jal moveStack
64
65              move $a0,$s0    # step 2:
66              move $a1,$s1
67              jal moveRing    # move a ring to destination
68
69              move $a0,$s2    # step 3:
70              move $a1,$s1
71              move $a2,$s0    # source = spare
```

```
72              jal moveStack
73
74              j end
75      moveOne:
76              jal moveRing      # Move one ring only
77
78      end:    lw $a0,0($sp)     # restore registers
79              lw $a1,4($sp)
80              lw $a2,8($sp)
81              lw $a3,12($sp)
82              lw $s0,16($sp)
83              lw $s1,20($sp)
84              lw $s2,24($sp)
85              lw $ra,28($sp)
86              add $sp,$sp,32
87              jr $ra
88
89      #------------------------------------------------
90      # moveRing - move one ring from source to dest
91      #       a0 - source
92      #       a1 - dest
93      #       t0 - holds the value removed
94      #------------------------------------------------
95      moveRing:
96              sub $sp,$sp,12    # save registers on stack
97              sw $a0,0($sp)
98              sw $a1,4($sp)
99              sw $ra,8($sp)
100
101             jal PrintTowers # print out state of towers
102
103     finds:  sub $a0,$a0,4    # get the top ring
104             lw $t0,($a0)
105             beqz $t0,founds
106             j finds          # find source
107     founds: add $a0,$a0,4
108
109             lw $t0,($a0)      # t0 holds the value removed
110             sw $0,($a0)       # set place to zero
111
112     findd:  sub $a1,$a1,4    # find destination
113             lw $t1,($a1)
114             beqz $t1,foundd
115             j findd
116     foundd: sw $t0,($a1)      # destination found
117
```

```
118             lw $a0,0($sp)     # restore registers
119             lw $a1,4($sp)
120             lw $ra,8($sp)
121             add $sp,$sp,12
122
123             jr $ra
124
125     #-----------------------------------------------
126     # PrintTowers - print out state of towers
127     #       s0 - number of rings
128     #       s1 - tower1
129     #       s2 - tower2
130     #       s3 - tower3
131     #-----------------------------------------------
132     PrintTowers:
133             sub $sp,$sp,28    # save registers on stack
134             sw $v0,0($sp)
135             sw $a0,4($sp)
136             sw $s0,8($sp)
137             sw $s1,12($sp)
138             sw $s2,16($sp)
139             sw $s3,20($sp)
140             sw $ra,24($sp)
141
142             la $s1,tower1     # set up the registers
143             la $s2,tower2     # from the data segment
144             la $s3,tower3
145             lw $s0,numRings
146
147             mul $s0,$s0,4     # each word four bytes
148             sub $s1,$s1,$s0   # get stacks ready
149             sub $s2,$s2,$s0
150             sub $s3,$s3,$s0
151
152     Loop:   beqz $s0,exit     # if at level -n done
153             la $a0,Blanks
154             li $v0,4          # system call to print
155             syscall           # out a string
156
157             lw $a0,($s1)      # read number on stack 1
158             jal printOne      # print blank or ring
159             lw $a0,($s2)      # read number on stack 2
160             jal printOne      # print blank or ring
161             lw $a0,($s3)      # read number on stack 3
162             jal printOne      # print blank or ring
163
```

```
164             la $a0,endl      # end line
165             li $v0,4         # system call to print
166             syscall          # out a string
167
168             sub $s0,$s0,4    # move up to next level
169             add $s1,$s1,4
170             add $s2,$s2,4
171             add $s3,$s3,4
172             j Loop           # repeat until $s0=0
173
174     exit:   la $a0,Base      # print Tower names and lines
175             li $v0,4         # system call to print
176             syscall          # out a string
177
178             lw $v0,0($sp)    # restore registers
179             lw $a0,4($sp)
180             lw $s0,8($sp)
181             lw $s1,12($sp)
182             lw $s2,16($sp)
183             lw $s3,20($sp)
184             lw $ra,24($sp)
185             add $sp,$sp,28
186             jr $ra
187
188
189     #------------------------------------------------
190     # printOne - print blank or ring number
191     #       a0 - holds ring number or 0
192     #       v0 - parameter for system call
193     #------------------------------------------------
194
195     printOne:
196             sub $sp,$sp,12    # save registers on stack
197             sw $a0,0($sp)
198             sw $v0,4($sp)
199             sw $ra,8($sp)
200
201             bnez $a0,ring    # if not zero then print it
202             la $a0,Blank
203             li $v0,4         # system call to print
204             syscall          # out a string
205
206             j spaces
207     ring:   li $v0,1         # print number
208             syscall
209
```

```
210    spaces:  la $a0,Blanks    # space output out
211             li $v0,4          # system call to print
212             syscall           # out a string
213
214             lw $a0,0($sp)     # restore registers
215             lw $v0,4($sp)
216             lw $ra,8($sp)
217             add $sp,$sp,12
218             jr $ra
219
220    ####################################################
221    #                                                  #
222    #                 data segment                     #
223    #                                                  #
224    ####################################################
225
226             .data
227    Blanks:  .asciiz "           "
228    Blank:   .asciiz " "
229    endl:    .asciiz "\n"
230    Base:    .ascii  "    ____    ____    ____\n"
231             .asciiz "     T1      T2      T3\n\n\n"
232
233
234             .align 2
235    notused:
236             .word 0,0,0,0,0,0,0,1,2,3
237    tower1:  .word 0,0,0,0,0,0,0,0,0,0
238    tower2:  .word 0,0,0,0,0,0,0,0,0,0
239    tower3:  .word 0
240    numRings:
241             .word 3
242
243    ##
244    ## end of file hanoi.a
```

The procedures in the program expect that stacks (representing stacks of rings on towers) are represented in the usual way for MIPS, with the base of the stack at the high-address end of the area that has been set aside for the stack (lines 234–239) of hanoi.a.

When the stack is empty, the top of the stack is identical with the base, and is an address just outside the allocated area. Stacks of rings will be represented as stacks of integers, in which the integer zero means 'no ring'.

The procedure printOne either writes a ring number or leaves blank spaces if there is no ring in that position. PrintTowers repeatedly calls printOne to output the present state of all three towers.

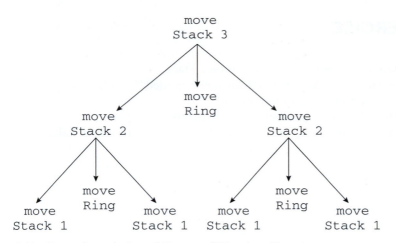

Figure 8.12 Recursive solution of Towers of Hanoi problem.

Procedure `moveRing` moves a ring from one tower to another. It calls `PrintTowers` so that each change in the state is displayed in the output as it occurs.

The recursive procedure that solves the Towers of Hanoi problem is called `moveStack` (Figure 8.12). It recursively moves the top $n - 1$ rings from the source tower to the spare tower, using the end tower as the spare. It then calls `moveRing` to move the bottom ring from the start tower to the destination tower. `moveRing` also prints out the new state of the towers. Finally, `moveStack` recursively moves the $n - 1$ rings from the spare tower to the destination tower, using the source tower as the spare.

8.9 SUMMARY

A stack of data elements is a last in, first out data structure. The MIPS stack is upside down – elements are added at progressively lower memory addresses. Procedures allow programs to be broken into smaller more manageable units. The jump and link instruction puts the return address into a special register before executing the code for the procedure. A procedure that calls another can count on callee saves being restored when control returns, but must save caller saves on the stack before making the call. Stack frames are used in procedure calls. The compiler figures out how big the frame needs to be, and the first thing it does in the body of the procedure is to allocate room on the stack for the frame. A recursive task is one that calls itself. With each invocation, the problem is reduced to a smaller problem until the task arrives at some terminal or base case which stops the process.

EXERCISES

8.1 What are the basic operations on a stack?

8.2 What is a stack frame and when is it needed?

8.3 Why are procedures important?

8.4 How do procedures get their arguments?

8.5 What convention is used by MIPS procedures to return values?

8.6 What are the advantages of caller and callee saves respectively?

8.7 Contrast the usage of registers and the stack for variables in procedures.

APPENDIX A

MIPS programming exams

A.1 INTRODUCTION

This appendix describes the MIPSMARK software, the basic idea behind which is to allow a lecturer to set assembly language programming questions and collect and mark the assignments automatically. MIPSMARK is written as a collection of Unix C shell scripts. Experience has shown that assessment defines the curriculum from the point of view of the student. If programming assignments are collected on printouts, they are often not taken seriously by students. In addition, automatically marked questions are ideal for teaching introductory computer architecture to very large class sizes. MIPSMARK would also allow any reader of the book to run MIPS assembly code against several test cases to determine if it works correctly.

The vision behind MIPSMARK is that the only way to learn introductory programming is via mastery of the techniques of writing simple programs. The student must develop the necessary reasoning and problem solving modes of thinking, as well as being able to use the software tools, to get a program to work correctly. While it may seem unfair to give zero for a program that 'nearly' works, this approach is essential to ensure that programming skills are developed. All the MIPSMARK exams are open book and the questions will be closely related to examples from notes and textbooks, therefore every student will be able to type in something with a reasonable resemblance to the answer. In open book exams of this type, it is meaningless to award marks for attempts that resemble the correct answer. Included with MIPSMARK is a large number of MIPS programming questions which allows a user to write a MIPS program and have it marked automatically.

A.2 MIPSMARK SOFTWARE

This section describes the MIPSMARK software for correcting assembly language programs. MIPSMARK works by running a program and searching for a precise sequence of characters in the output. This is called 'black box testing'. You must therefore follow the instructions exactly to produce this sequence of characters or your program will not get any marks. Your output must be ASCII text. Any non-ASCII or unusual control characters in your output means MIPSMARK may not find the answer. If you like, you can put a carriage return at the end of the required output.

You must not change the filenames because these are used to match the test cases with the questions. Your program must not prompt for any input as it will be run and marked automatically.

easy.a shows the format of an exam question.

```
 1    ## Start of file easy.a
 2    ##
 3    ## Question:
 4    ## Print out the message "hello world"
 5    ##
 6    ## Output format must be:
 7    ## "hello world"
 8
 9    #################################################
10    #                                               #
11    #                 text segment                  #
12    #                                               #
13    #################################################
14
15            .text
16            .globl __start
17    __start:                # execution starts here
18
19
20    # Any changes above this line will be discarded by
21    # mipsmark. Put your answer between dashed lines.
22    #------------ start cut -------------------------
23
24
25
26    #------------  end cut  -------------------------
27    # Any changes below this line will be discarded by
28    # mipsmark. Put your answer between dashed lines.
29
```

```
30     #################################################
31     #                                               #
32     #                data segment                   #
33     #                                               #
34     #################################################
35
36             .data
37     str:    .asciiz "hello world\n"
38     ##
39     ## End of file easy.a
```

You should type the answer between the dashed lines as indicated. Test your code by loading the file into XSPIM and running it. Once you are satisfied with the solution type mipsmark file.a in a terminal window. In general, **MIPSMARK** works by extracting your answer from between the dashed lines and trying it using several different test cases as shown in Figure A.1. easy.a is a simple program that needs only one test case.

If your program works for case zero and case one, but fails for case two you can get a copy of the source code for the third test case by typing showcase file.a 2, which will give you a file called file_2.a. Use the programming tools to locate the bug in your code preventing this test case from working correctly.

Of course, it is possible to get your program to pass the **MIPSMARK** program by explicitly writing out the correct answers to each test case! To overcome this problem, when your program is being marked in an exam, additional test cases have to be used. To test your code fully, you can add your own test cases in the data segement and verify that these also work, but remember that when the program is being marked by **MIPSMARK**, anything outside the dashed lines will be discarded.

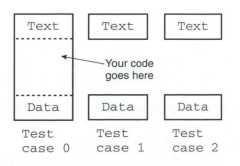

Figure A.1 Automatically corrected programs.

A.3   EXAM QUESTIONS USING PROGRAM

LOOPS

This section shows some example programs that test your knowledge of looping programs.

A.3.1   QUESTION LOOP2

```
 1    ## Start of file loop2.a
 2    ##
 3    ## Question:
 4    ## calculate the number of occurrences of "letter"
 5    ## in the string "chararray"
 6    ##
 7    ## Output format must be:
 8    ## "number of occurrences = 6"
 9
10    ################################################
11    #                                              #
12    #              text segment                    #
13    #                                              #
14    ################################################
15
16            .text
17            .globl __start
18    __start:                    # execution starts here
19
20
21    # Any changes above this line will be discarded by
22    # mipsmark. Put your answer between dashed lines.
23    #------------ start cut --------------------------
24
25
26
27    #------------ end cut   --------------------------
28    # Any changes below this line will be discarded by
29    # mipsmark. Put your answer between dashed lines.
30
31    ################################################
32    #                                              #
33    #              data segment                    #
34    #                                              #
35    ################################################
```

```
36
37          .data
38   chararray:
39          .asciiz "abbbaabbbababab"
40   letter: .byte 'a'
41   ans:    .asciiz "number of occurences = "
42   endl:   .asciiz "\n"
43   ##
44   ## End of file loop2.a
```

A.3.2   QUESTION LOOP7

```
1    ## Start of file loop7.a
2    ##
3    ## Question:
4    ## Replace the first and last character in the
5    ## string "charstr" with 'X'.
6    ##
7    ## Then print the resulting string.
8    ##
9    ## Output format must be:
10   ## "XbcdeX"
11
12   ####################################################
13   #                                                  #
14   #                text segment                      #
15   #                                                  #
16   ####################################################
17
18          .text
19          .globl __start
20   __start:                   # execution starts here
21
22
23   # Any changes above this line will be discarded by
24   # mipsmark. Put your answer between dashed lines.
25   #------------ start cut -------------------------
26
27
28
29   #------------ end cut  --------------------------
30   # Any changes below this line will be discarded by
31   # mipsmark. Put your answer between dashed lines.
32
```

```
33      ################################################
34      #                                              #
35      #              data segment                    #
36      #                                              #
37      ################################################
38
39              .data
40      charstr:
41              .asciiz "abcdef"
42      endl:   .asciiz "\n"
43      ##
44      ## End of file loop7.a
```

A.3.3   QUESTION LOOP8

```
1       ## Start of file loop8.a
2       ##
3       ## Question:
4       ## Replace the last character in the
5       ## string "charstr" with the first character.
6       ##
7       ## Then print the resulting string.
8       ##
9       ## Output format must be:
10      ## "abcdea"
11
12      ################################################
13      #                                              #
14      #              text segment                    #
15      #                                              #
16      ################################################
17
18              .text
19              .globl __start
20      __start:                    # execution starts here
21
22
23      # Any changes above this line will be discarded by
24      # mipsmark. Put your answer between dashed lines.
25      #----------- start cut ------------------------
26
27
28
29      #----------- end cut   ------------------------
30      # Any changes below this line will be discarded by
```

```
31     # mipsmark. Put your answer between dashed lines.
32
33     #################################################
34     #                                               #
35     #                data segment                   #
36     #                                               #
37     #################################################
38
39             .data
40     charstr:
41             .asciiz "abcdef"
42       endl: .asciiz "\n"
43     ##
44     ## End of file loop8.a
```

A.3.4   QUESTION LOOP9

```
 1     ## Start of file loop9.a
 2     ##
 3     ## Question:
 4     ## Replace the second last character in the
 5     ## string "charstr" with the last character.
 6     ## The string will contain at least 2 characters.
 7     ##
 8     ## Then print the resulting string.
 9     ##
10     ## Output format must be:
11     ## "abcdff"
12
13     #################################################
14     #                                               #
15     #                text segment                   #
16     #                                               #
17     #################################################
18
19             .text
20             .globl __start
21     __start:                 # execution starts here
22
23
24     # Any changes above this line will be discarded by
25     # mipsmark. Put your answer between dashed lines.
26     #------------ start cut -------------------------
27
28
```

```
29
30    #------------ end cut  -------------------------
31    # Any changes below this line will be discarded by
32    # mipsmark. Put your answer between dashed lines.
33
34    ################################################
35    #                                              #
36    #               data segment                   #
37    #                                              #
38    ################################################
39
40            .data
41    charstr:
42            .asciiz "abcdef"
43    endl:   .asciiz "\n"
44    ##
45    ## End of file loop9.a
```

A.3.5   QUESTION LOOPA

```
1     ## Start of file loopa.a
2     ##
3     ## Question:
4     ## Replace the first character in the
5     ## string "charstr" with the last character.
6     ## The string will contain at least 2 characters.
7     ##
8     ## Then print the resulting string.
9     ##
10    ## Output format must be:
11    ## "fbcdef"
12
13    ################################################
14    #                                              #
15    #               text segment                   #
16    #                                              #
17    ################################################
18
19            .text
20            .globl __start
21    __start:                    # execution starts here
22
23
24    # Any changes above this line will be discarded by
25    # mipsmark. Put your answer between dashed lines.
```

```
26    #------------ start cut ------------------------
27
28
29
30    #------------ end cut   ------------------------
31    # Any changes below this line will be discarded by
32    # mipsmark. Put your answer between dashed lines.
33
34    #################################################
35    #                                               #
36    #                data segment                   #
37    #                                               #
38    #################################################
39
40            .data
41    charstr:
42            .asciiz "abcdef"
43    endl:   .asciiz "\n"
44    ##
45    ## End of file loopa.a
```

A.3.6   QUESTION TCOMP

```
1     ## Start of file tcomp.a
2     ##
3     ## Question:
4     ## Print the absolute value of the element in
5     ## "array" with the largest absolute value.
6     ## "count" holds the number of elements in "array"
7     ##
8     ## Output format must be:
9     ## "max absolute value is = 43"
10
11    #################################################
12    #                                               #
13    #                text segment                   #
14    #                                               #
15    #################################################
16
17            .text
18            .globl __start
19    __start:                    # execution starts here
20
21
22    # Any changes above this line will be discarded by
```

```
23    # mipsmark. Put your answer between dashed lines.
24    #------------ start cut -------------------------
25
26
27
28    #------------  end cut  -------------------------
29    # Any changes below this line will be discarded by
30    # mipsmark. Put your answer between dashed lines.
31
32    ################################################
33    #                                              #
34    #              data segment                    #
35    #                                              #
36    ################################################
37
38            .data
39    array:  .word 3,0xffffffd5,2,6
40    count:  .word 4
41    ans1:   .asciiz "max absolute value is = "
42    endl:   .asciiz "\n"
43    ##
44    ## End of file tcomp.a
```

A.3.7   QUESTION TCOMP1

```
 1    ## Start of file tcomp1.a
 2    ##
 3    ## Question:
 4    ## calculate the sum of the elements in "array"
 5    ## whose absolute value is greater than forty
 6    ## "count" holds the number of elements in "array"
 7    ##
 8    ## Output format must be:
 9    ## "sum is = -60"
10
11    ################################################
12    #                                              #
13    #              text segment                    #
14    #                                              #
15    ################################################
16
17            .text
18            .globl __start
19    __start:                    # execution starts here
20
```

```
21
22    # Any changes above this line will be discarded by
23    # mipsmark. Put your answer between dashed lines.
24    #------------ start cut -------------------------
25
26
27
28    #------------ end cut   -------------------------
29    # Any changes below this line will be discarded by
30    # mipsmark. Put your answer between dashed lines.
31
32    ################################################
33    #                                              #
34    #                 data segment                 #
35    #                                              #
36    ################################################
37
38          .data
39    array:  .word 3,0xfffffffd5,2,6,50,-67
40    count:  .word 6
41    ans1:   .asciiz "sum is = "
42    endl:   .asciiz "\n"
43    ##
44    ## End of file tcomp1.a
```

A.4   EXAM QUESTION USING BIT MANIPULATION

This section shows an example program that tests your knowledge of the logical, shift and rotate instructions.

A.4.1   QUESTION LOGIC3

```
1    ## Start of file logic3.a
2    ##
3    ## Question:
4    ## "number" is a word.
5    ## If bits 3 and 6 are set then
6    ## set bits 0, 1 and 2 and print out
7    ## the result.
```

```
 8     ## If bits 3 and 6 are not set then
 9     ## print out the number unchanged.
10     ##
11     ## Output format must be:
12     ## "result is = 79"
13
14     #################################################
15     #                                               #
16     #                text segment                   #
17     #                                               #
18     #################################################
19
20             .text
21             .globl __start
22     __start:                # execution starts here
23
24
25     # Any changes above this line will be discarded by
26     # mipsmark. Put your answer between dashed lines.
27     #------------ start cut ------------------------
28
29
30
31     #------------   end cut   ----------------------
32     # Any changes below this line will be discarded by
33     # mipsmark. Put your answer between dashed lines.
34
35     #################################################
36     #                                               #
37     #                data segment                   #
38     #                                               #
39     #################################################
40
41             .data
42     number: .word 0x48
43     ans:    .asciiz "result is = "
44     endl:   .asciiz "\n"
45     ##
46     ## End of file logic3.a
```

A.5   EXAM QUESTIONS USING THE STACK

This section shows some example programs that test your ability to use the stack data structure.

A.5.1   QUESTION STACK2

```
1     ## Start of file stack2.a
2     ##
3     ## Question:
4     ## The program must sum a sequence of numbers
5     ## stored on the stack. The word
6     ## on the top of the stack tells you how
7     ## many numbers are in the sequence.
8     ## Do not include this first word in the sum.
9     ##
10    ## Do not rely on the existence of the "test"
11    ## variable, or the code above the
12    ## dashed line.
13    ##
14    ## Output format must be:
15    ## "sum is = 23"
16
17    #################################################
18    #                                               #
19    #                text segment                   #
20    #                                               #
21    #################################################
22
23            .text
24            .globl __start
25    __start:                # execution starts here
26
27            la $t0,test     # This code sets up the stack
28            lw $t1,($t0)    # Do not alter
29            add $t0,$t0,4
30    loop:   lw $t2,($t0)
31            sub $sp,$sp,4
32            sw $t2,($sp)
33            add $t0,$t0,4
34            add $t1,$t1,-1
35            bnez $t1,loop
36            la $t0,test
37            lw $t1,($t0)
38            sub $sp,$sp,4
39            sw $t1,($sp)
40
41                            # Stack set up now....
42
43    # Any changes above this line will be discarded by
44    # mipsmark. Put your answer between dashed lines.
```

```
45    #------------ start cut -------------------------
46
47
48
49    #------------ end cut  -------------------------
50    # Any changes below this line will be discarded by
51    # mipsmark. Put your answer between dashed lines.
52          :
53    #################################################
54    #                                               #
55    #              data segment                     #
56    #                                               #
57    #################################################
58
59            .data
60    test:   .word 4,6,7,8,2
61    ans:    .asciiz "sum is = "
62    endl:   .asciiz "\n"
63    ##
64    ## End of file stack2.a
```

A.5.2   QUESTION STACK3

```
1     ## Start of file stack3.a
2     ##
3     ## Question:
4     ## The program must sum a sequence of numbers
5     ## stored on the stack. "num"
6     ## tells you how many numbers are in the sequence.
7     ##
8     ## Do not rely on the existence of the "test"
9     ## variable, or the code above the
10    ## dashed line.
11    ##
12
13    ## Output format must be:
14    ## "sum is = 15"
15
16    #################################################
17    #                                               #
18    #              text segment                     #
19    #                                               #
20    #################################################
21
22            .text
23            .globl __start
```

```
24    __start:                    # execution starts here
25
26            la $t0,test         # This code sets up the stack
27            lw $t1,num
28    loop:   lw $t2,($t0)
29            sub $sp,$sp,4
30            sw $t2,($sp)
31            add $t0,$t0,4
32            add $t1,$t1,-1
33            bnez $t1,loop
34
35                                # Stack set up now....
36
37    # Any changes above this line will be discarded by
38    # mipsmark. Put your answer between dashed lines.
39    #------------ start cut --------------------------
40
41
42
43    #------------ end cut  --------------------------
44    # Any changes below this line will be discarded by
45    # mipsmark. Put your answer between dashed lines.
46
47    #################################################
48    #                                               #
49    #                 data segment                  #
50    #                                               #
51    #################################################
52
53            .data
54    test:   .word 4,-6,7,8,2
55    num:    .word 5
56    ans:    .asciiz "sum is = "
57    endl:   .asciiz "\n"
58    ##
59    ## End of file stack3.a
```

A.5.3   QUESTION STACK4

```
1     ## Start of file stack4.a
2     ##
3     ## Question:
4     ## The program must find the smallest number in
5     ## a sequence of ten numbers stored on the stack.
6     ##
```

```
 7    ## Do not rely on the existence of the "test"
 8    ## variable, or the code above the
 9    ## dashed line.
10    ##
11
12    ## Output format must be:
13    ## "min is = -8"
14
15    ################################################
16    #                                              #
17    #                text segment                  #
18    #                                              #
19    ################################################
20
21            .text
22            .globl __start
23    __start:                    # execution starts here
24
25            la $t0,test     # This code sets up the stack
26            li $t1,10
27    loop:   lw $t2,($t0)
28            sub $sp,$sp,4
29            sw $t2,($sp)
30            add $t0,$t0,4
31            add $t1,$t1,-1
32            bnez $t1,loop
33
34                                # Stack set up now....
35
36    # Any changes above this line will be discarded by
37    # mipsmark. Put your answer between dashed lines.
38    #------------ start cut --------------------------
39
40
41
42    #------------ end cut  ---------------------------
43    # Any changes below this line will be discarded by
44    # mipsmark. Put your answer between dashed lines.
45
46    ################################################
47    #                                              #
48    #                data segment                  #
49    #                                              #
50    ################################################
51
52            .data
```

```
53    test:   .word 4,-6,7,8,0,6,6,-8,6,6
54    ans:    .asciiz "min is = "
55    endl:   .asciiz "\n"
56    ##
57    ## End of file stack4.a
```

A.5.4   QUESTION STACK5

```
1     ## Start of file stack5.a
2     ##
3     ## Question:
4     ## The program must sum numbers
5     ## stored on the stack
6     ## that have bit 6 set.
7     ## The word
8     ## on the top of the stack tells you how
9     ## many numbers are in the sequence.
10    ## Do not include this first word in the sum.
11    ##
12    ## Do not rely on the existence of the "test"
13    ## variable, or the code above the
14    ## dashed line.
15    ##
16    ## Output format must be:
17    ## "sum is = 169"
18
19    ##################################################
20    #                                                #
21    #                text segment                    #
22    #                                                #
23    ##################################################
24
25            .text
26            .globl __start
27    __start:                  # execution starts here
28
29            la $t0,test        # This code sets up the stack
30            lw $t1,($t0)       # Do not alter
31            add $t0,$t0,4
32    loop:   lw $t2,($t0)
33            sub $sp,$sp,4
34            sw $t2,($sp)
35            add $t0,$t0,4
36            add $t1,$t1,-1
37            bnez $t1,loop
```

```
38            la $t0,test
39            lw $t1,($t0)
40            sub $sp,$sp,4
41            sw $t1,($sp)
42
43                              # Stack set up now....
44
45   # Any changes above this line will be discarded by
46   # mipsmark. Put your answer between dashed lines.
47   #------------ start cut -------------------------
48
49
50
51   #------------ end cut  -------------------------
52   # Any changes below this line will be discarded by
53   # mipsmark. Put your answer between dashed lines.
54
55   ################################################
56   #                                              #
57   #              data segment                    #
58   #                                              #
59   ################################################
60
61         .data
62   test:  .word 4,0x96,0x47,0x28,0x62
63   ans:   .asciiz "sum is = "
64   endl:  .asciiz "\n"
65   ##
66   ## End of file stack5.a
```

A.5.5   QUESTION STACK7

```
1    ## Start of file stack7.a
2    ##
3    ## Question:
4    ##
5    ## Pop the stack until a
6    ## word is found which if printed out
7    ## in hex would contain a "C", and print
8    ## out that word in decimal.
9    ##
10   ## Do not rely on the existence of the "test"
11   ## or "num" variables, or the code above the
12   ## dashed line.
13   ##
```

```
14      ## Output format must be:
15      ## "Number is = 192"
16
17      ##################################################
18      #                                                #
19      #                text segment                    #
20      #                                                #
21      ##################################################
22
23              .text
24              .globl __start
25      __start:                    # execution starts here
26
27              la $t0,test         # This code sets up the stack
28              lw $t1,num          # Do not alter
29      loop:   lw $t2,($t0)
30              sub $sp,$sp,4
31              sw $t2,($sp)
32              add $t0,$t0,4
33              add $t1,$t1,-1
34              bnez $t1,loop
35                                  # Stack set up now....
36
37      # Any changes above this line will be discarded by
38      # mipsmark. Put your answer between dashed lines.
39      #------------ start cut -------------------------
40
41
42
43      #------------  end cut  -------------------------
44      # Any changes below this line will be discarded by
45      # mipsmark. Put your answer between dashed lines.
46
47      ##################################################
48      #                                                #
49      #                data segment                    #
50      #                                                #
51      ##################################################
52
53              .data
54      test:   .word 0x99,0xc0,0xf,0xa,1,0xd
55      num:    .word 6
56      ans:    .asciiz "Number is = "
57      endl:   .asciiz "\n"
58      ##
59      ## End of file stack7.a
```

A.6   EXAM QUESTIONS USING FUNCTIONS

This section shows some example programs that test your ability to use the MIPS function call mechanism.

A.6.1   QUESTION FUNCT3

```
 1    ## Start of file funct3.a
 2    ##
 3    ## Question:
 4    ## Write a function "setbits" that takes a
 5    ## number in $a0 and sets all the bits from
 6    ## the most significant bit down.
 7    ## Return the resulting number in the register $v0.
 8    ## For example 100111 base two becomes 111111.
 9    ##
10    ## Output format must be:
11    ## "Number is = 63"
12
13    ##################################################
14    #                                                #
15    #              text segment                      #
16    #                                                #
17    ##################################################
18
19            .text
20            .globl __start
21    __start:                    # execution starts here
22
23
24            la $a0,ans
25            li $v0,4
26            syscall
27
28            li $a0,39
29            jal setbits     # call function
30
31            move $a0,$v0
32            li $v0,1
33            syscall
34
35            la $a0,endl      # system call to print
36            li $v0,4         # out a newline
37            syscall
38
```

```
39    exit:     li $v0,10
40              syscall           # au revoir...
41
42    # Any changes above this line will be discarded by
43    # mipsmark. Put your answer between dashed lines.
44    #------------ start cut --------------------------
45
46
47
48    #------------ end cut  ---------------------------
49    # Any changes below this line will be discarded by
50    # mipsmark. Put your answer between dashed lines.
51
52    #################################################
53    #                                               #
54    #             data segment                      #
55    #                                               #
56    #################################################
57
58              .data
59    ans:      .asciiz "Number is = "
60    endl:     .asciiz "\n"
61    ##
62    ## End of file funct3.a
```

A.6.2   QUESTION FUNCT4

```
1     ## Start of file funct4.a
2     ##
3     ## Question:
4     ## Write a function "findpat" that takes a
5     ## long binary pattern in $a0 and a smaller
6     ## binary pattern in $a1, and returns true
7     ## if the long binary pattern contains the
8     ## smaller one.
9     ## For example 100111 base two contains 1001.
10    ##
11    ## Output format must be:
12    ## "Pattern found"
13
14    #################################################
15    #                                               #
16    #             text segment                      #
17    #                                               #
18    #################################################
19
```

```
20              .text
21              .globl __start
22      __start:                    # execution starts here
23

24

25              li $a0,39
26              li $a1,9
27              jal findpat     # call  function
28

29              beqz $v0,notthere
30

31              la $a0,yes
32              li $v0,4
33              syscall
34              b exit
35

36      notthere:
37              la $a0,no
38              li $v0,4
39              syscall
40

41      exit:   li $v0,10
42              syscall         # au revoir...
43

44      # Any changes above this line will be discarded by
45      # mipsmark. Put your answer between dashed lines.
46      #------------ start cut -------------------------
47

48

49

50      #------------  end cut  -------------------------
51      # Any changes below this line will be discarded by
52      # mipsmark. Put your answer between dashed lines.
53

54      ################################################
55      #                                              #
56      #            data segment                      #
57      #                                              #
58      ################################################
59

60              .data
61      yes:    .asciiz "Pattern found\n"
62      no:     .asciiz "Pattern not found\n"
63

64      ##
65      ## End of file funct4.a
```

A.6.3   QUESTION FUNCT5

```
1    ## Start of file funct5.a
2    ##
3    ## Question:
4    ## Write a function "check3" that takes a
5    ## number in $a0 and returns that number if
6    ## three consecutive bits are set. Otherwise
7    ## it returns zero.
8    ##
9    ## Output format must be:
10   ## "Number is = 39"
11
12   #################################################
13   #                                               #
14   #                text segment                   #
15   #                                               #
16   #################################################
17
18           .text
19           .globl __start
20   __start:                    # execution starts here
21
22
23           la $a0,ans
24           li $v0,4
25           syscall
26
27           li $a0,39
28           jal check3      # call  function
29
30           move $a0,$v0
31           li $v0,1
32           syscall
33
34           la $a0,endl      # system call to print
35           li $v0,4         # out a newline
36           syscall
37
38   exit:   li $v0,10
39           syscall          # au revoir...
40
41   # Any changes above this line will be discarded by
42   # mipsmark. Put your answer between dashed lines.
43   #----------- start cut -------------------------
```

```
44
45
46
47     #------------  end cut  --------------------------
48     # Any changes below this line will be discarded by
49     # mipsmark. Put your answer between dashed lines.
50
51     ##################################################
52     #                                                #
53     #               data segment                     #
54     #                                                #
55     ##################################################
56
57             .data
58     ans:    .asciiz "Number is = "
59     endl:   .asciiz "\n"
60     ##
61     ## End of file funct5.a
```

MIPS/SPIM instruction quick reference

This appendix contains a quick reference for the MIPS/SPIM instruction set, grouped together by instruction type. The † symbol denotes a pseudo-instruction.

Table B.1   Arithmetic and logical instructions.

Description	Opcode	Operands		
Absolute value	abs†	Rdest,	Rsrc	
Addition (with overflow)	add	Rdest,	Rsrc1,	Src2
Addition immediate (with overflow)	addi	Rdest,	Rsrc1,	Imm
Addition (without overflow)	addu	Rdest,	Rsrc1,	Src2
Addition immediate (without overflow)	addiu	Rdest,	Rsrc1,	Imm
AND	and	Rdest,	Rsrc1,	Src2
AND immediate	andi	Rdest,	Rsrc1,	Imm
Divide (signed)	div	Rsrc1,	Rsrc2	
Divide (unsigned)	divu	Rsrc1,	Rsrc2	
Divide (signed, with overflow)	div†	Rdest,	Rsrc1,	Src2
Divide (unsigned, without overflow)	divu†	Rdest,	Rsrc1,	Src2
Multiply (without overflow)	mul†	Rdest,	Rsrc1,	Src2
Multiply (with overflow)	mulo†	Rdest,	Rsrc1,	Src2
Unsigned multiply (with overflow)	mulou†	Rdest,	Rsrc1,	Src2
Multiply	mult	Rsrc1,	Rsrc2	
Unsigned multiply	multu	Rsrc1,	Rsrc2	
Negate value (with overflow)	neg†	Rdest,	Rsrc	
Negate value (without overflow)	negu†	Rdest,	Rsrc	
NOR	nor	Rdest,	Rsrc1,	Src2
NOT	not†	Rdest,	Rsrc	
OR	or	Rdest,	Rsrc1,	Src2
OR immediate	ori	Rdest,	Rsrc1,	Imm
Remainder	rem†	Rdest,	Rsrc1,	Src2

Table B.1 – continued

Description	Opcode	Operands
Unsigned remainder	remu†	Rdest, Rsrc1, Src2
Rotate left	rol†	Rdest, Rsrc1, Src2
Rotate right	ror†	Rdest, Rsrc1, Src2
Shift left logical	sll	Rdest, Rsrc1, Src2
Shift left logical variable	sllv	Rdest, Rsrc1, Rsrc2
Shift right arithmetic	sra	Rdest, Rsrc1, Src2
Shift right arithmetic variable	srav	Rdest, Rsrc1, Rsrc2
Shift right logical	srl	Rdest, Rsrc1, Src2
Shift right logical variable	srlv	Rdest, Rsrc1, Rsrc2
Subtract (with overflow)	sub	Rdest, Rsrc1, Src2
Subtract (without overflow)	subu	Rdest, Rsrc1, Src2
XOR	xor	Rdest, Rsrc1, Src2
XOR immediate	xori	Rdest, Rsrc1, Imm

Table B.2 Branch and jump instructions.

Description	Opcode	Operands
Branch instruction	b	label
Branch coprocessor z true	bczt	label
Branch coprocessor z false	bczf	label
Branch on equal	beq	Rsrc1, Src2, label
Branch on equal zero	beqz†	Rsrc, label
Branch on greater than equal	bge†	Rsrc1, Src2, label
Branch on GTE unsigned	bgeu†	Rsrc1, Src2, label
Branch on greater than equal zero	bgez	Rsrc, label
Branch on greater than equal zero and link	bgezal	Rsrc, label
Branch on greater than	bgt†	Rsrc1, Src2, label
Branch on greater than unsigned	bgtu†	Rsrc1, Src2, label
Branch on greater than zero	bgtz	Rsrc, label
Branch on less than equal	ble†	Rsrc1, Src2, label
Branch on LTE unsigned	bleu†	Rsrc1, Src2, label
Branch on less than equal zero	blez	Rsrc, label
Branch on greater than equal zero and link	bgezal	Rsrc, label
Branch on less than and link	bltzal	Rsrc, label
Branch on less than	blt†	Rsrc1, Src2, label
Branch on less than unsigned	bltu†	Rsrc1, Src2, label
Branch on less than zero	bltz	Rsrc, label
Branch on not equal	bne	Rsrc1, Src2, label
Branch on not equal zero	bnez†	Rsrc, label
Jump	j	label
Jump and link	jal	label
Jump and link register	jalr	Rsrc
Jump register	jr	Rsrc

Table B.3 Data movement instructions.

Description	Opcode	Operands
Move	move[†]	Rdest, Rsrc
Move from hi	mfhi	Rdest
Move from lo	mflo	Rdest
Move to hi	mthi	Rdest
Move to lo	mtlo	Rdest
Move from coprocessor z	mfcz	Rdest, CPsrc
Move double from coprocessor 1	mfc1.d[†]	Rdest, FRsrc1
Move to coprocessor z	mtcz	Rsrc, CPdest

Table B.4 Comparison instructions.

Description	Opcode	Operands
Set equal	seq[†]	Rdest, Rsrc1, Src2
Set greater than equal	sge[†]	Rdest, Rsrc1, Src2
Set greater than equal unsigned	sgeu[†]	Rdest, Rsrc1, Src2
Set greater than	sgt[†]	Rdest, Rsrc1, Src2
Set greater than unsigned	sgtu[†]	Rdest, Rsrc1, Src2
Set less than equal	sle[†]	Rdest, Rsrc1, Src2
Set less than equal unsigned	sleu[†]	Rdest, Rsrc1, Src2
Set less than	slt	Rdest, Rsrc1, Src2
Set less than immediate	slti	Rdest, Rsrc1, Imm
Set less than unsigned	sltu	Rdest, Rsrc1, Src2
Set less than unsigned immediate	sltiu	Rdest, Rsrc1, Imm
Set not equal	sne[†]	Rdest, Rsrc1, Src2

Table B.5 Constant-manipulating instructions.

Description	Opcode	Operands
Load immediate	li[†]	Rdest, imm
Load upper immediate	lui	Rdest, imm

Table B.6 Load instructions.

Description	Opcode	Operands
Load address	la†	Rdest, address
Load byte	lb	Rdest, address
Load unsigned byte	lbu	Rdest, address
Load double-word	ld†	Rdest, address
Load halfword	lh	Rdest, address
Load unsigned halfword	lhu	Rdest, address
Load word	lw	Rdest, address
Load word coprocessor	lwcz	Rdest, address
Load word left	lwl	Rdest, address
Load word right	lwr	Rdest, address
Unaligned load halfword	ulh†	Rdest, address
Unaligned load halfword unsigned	ulhu†	Rdest, address
Unaligned load word	ulw†	Rdest, address

Table B.7 Store instructions.

Description	Opcode	Operands
Store byte	sb	Rsrc, address
Store double-word	sd†	Rsrc, address
Store halfword	sh	Rsrc, address
Store word	sw	Rsrc, address
Store word coprocessor	swcz	Rsrc, address
Store word left	swl	Rsrc, address
Store word right	swr	Rsrc, address
Unaligned store halfword	ush†	Rsrc, address
Unaligned store word	usw†	Rsrc, address

Table B.8 Floating point instructions.

Description	Opcode	Operands
Floating point absolute value double	abs.d	FRdest, FRsrc
Floating point absolute value single	abs.s	FRdest, FRsrc
Floating point addition double	add.d	FRdest, FRsrc1, FRsrc2
Floating point addition single	add.s	FRdest, FRsrc1, FRsrc2
Compare equal double	c.eq.d	FRsrc1, FRsrc2
Compare equal single	c.eq.s	FRsrc1, FRsrc2
Compare less than equal double	c.le.d	FRsrc1, FRsrc2
Compare less than equal single	c.le.s	FRsrc1, FRsrc2
Compare less than double	c.lt.d	FRsrc1, FRsrc2
Compare less than single	c.lt.s	FRsrc1, FRsrc2
Convert single to double	cvt.d.s	FRdest, FRsrc
Convert integer to double	cvt.d.w	FRdest, FRsrc
Convert double to single	cvt.s.d	FRdest, FRsrc
Convert integer to single	cvt.s.w	FRdest, FRsrc
Convert double to integer	cvt.w.d	FRdest, FRsrc
Convert single to integer	cvt.w.s	FRdest, FRsrc
Floating point divide double	div.d	FRdest, FRsrc1, FRsrc2
Floating point divide single	div.s	FRdest, FRsrc1, FRsrc2
Load floating point double	l.d[†]	FRdest, address
Load floating point single	l.s.[†]	FRdest, address
Move floating point double	mov.d	FRdest, FRsrc
Move floating point single	mov.s	FRdest, FRsrc
Floating point multiply double	mul.d	FRdest, FRsrc1, FRsrc2
Floating point multiply single	mul.s	FRdest, FRsrc1, FRsrc2
Negate double	neg.d	FRdest, FRsrc
Negate single	neg.s	FRdest, FRsrc
Store floating point double	s.d[†]	FRdest, address
Store floating point single	s.s[†]	FRdest, address
Floating point subtract double	sub.d	FRdest, FRsrc1, FRsrc2
Floating point subtract single	sub.s	FRdest, FRsrc1, FRsrc2

Table B.9 Exception and trap instructions.

Description	Opcode	Operands
Return from exception	rfe	
System call	syscall	
Break	break	n
No operation	nop	

APPENDIX C

MIPS/SPIM instruction reference

The † symbol denotes a pseudo-instruction.

abs.d
Floating point absolute value double

```
abs.d FRdest, FRsrc
```

Compute the absolute value of the floating point double in register FRsrc and put it in register FRdest.

abs.s
Floating point absolute value single

```
abs.s FRdest, FRsrc
```

Compute the absolute value of the floating point single in register FRsrc and put it in register FRdest.

abs†
Absolute value

```
abs Rdest, Rsrc
```

Put the absolute value of the integer from register Rsrc in register Rdest.

add.d
Floating point addition double

```
add.d FRdest, FRsrc1, FRsrc2
```

Compute the sum of the floating point doubles in registers `FRsrc1` and `Frsrc2` and put it in register `FRdest`.

add.s
Floating point addition single

```
add.s FRdest, FRsrc1, FRsrc2
```

Compute the sum of the floating point singles in registers `FRsrc1` and `FRsrc2` and put it in register `FRdest`.

addiu
Addition immediate (without overflow)

```
addiu Rdest, Rsrc1, Imm
```

Put the sum of the integers from register `Rsrc1` and `Imm` into register `Rdest`.

addi
Addition immediate (with overflow)

```
addi Rdest, Rsrc1, Imm
```

Put the sum of the integers from register `Rsrc1` and `Imm` into register `Rdest`.

addu
Addition (without overflow)

```
addu Rdest, Rsrc1, Src2
```

Put the sum of the integers from register `Rsrc1` and `Src2` into register `Rdest`.

add
Addition (with overflow)

```
add Rdest, Rsrc1, Src2
```

Put the sum of the integers from register `Rsrc1` and `Src2` into register `Rdest`.

andi   AND immediate

```
andi Rdest, Rsrc1, Imm
```

Put the logical AND of the integers from register `Rsrc1` and `Imm` into register `Rdest`.

and   AND

```
and Rdest, Rsrc1, Src2
```

Put the logical AND of the integers from register `Rsrc1` and `Src2` into register `Rdest`.

bczf   Branch coprocessor z false

```
bczf label
```

Conditionally branch to the instruction at the label if coprocessor z's condition flag is false.

bczt   Branch coprocessor z true

```
bczt label
```

Conditionally branch to the instruction at the label if coprocessor z's condition flag is true.

beqz[†]   Branch on equal zero

```
beqz Rsrc, label
```

Conditionally branch to the instruction at the label if the contents of `Rsrc` equal 0.

beq
Branch on equal

```
beq Rsrc1, Src2, label
```

Conditionally branch to the instruction at the label if the contents of register Rsrc1 equals Src2.

bgeu†
Branch on GTE unsigned

```
bgeu Rsrc1, Src2, label
```

Conditionally branch to the instruction at the label if the contents of register Rsrc1 are greater than or equal to Src2.

bgezal
Branch on greater than equal zero and link

```
bgezal Rsrc, label
```

Conditionally branch to the instruction at the label if the contents of Rsrc are greater than or equal to 0. Save the address of the next instruction in register 31.

bgezal
Branch on greater than equal zero and link

```
bgezal Rsrc, label
```

Conditionally branch to the instruction at the label if the contents of Rsrc are greater than or equal to 0. Save the address of the next instruction in register 31.

bgez
Branch on greater than equal zero

```
bgez Rsrc, label
```

Conditionally branch to the instruction at the label if the contents of Rsrc are greater than or equal to 0.

bge†

Branch on greater than equal

    bge Rsrc1, Src2, label

Conditionally branch to the instruction at the label if the contents of register Rsrc1 are greater than or equal to Src2.

bgtu†

Branch on greater than unsigned

    bgtu Rsrc1, Src2, label

Conditionally branch to the instruction at the label if the contents of register Rsrc1 are greater than Src2.

bgtz

Branch on greater than zero

    bgtz Rsrc, label

Conditionally branch to the instruction at the label if the contents of Rsrc are greater than 0.

bgt†

Branch on greater than

    bgt Rsrc1, Src2, label

Conditionally branch to the instruction at the label if the contents of register Rsrc1 are greater than Src2.

bleu†

Branch on LTE unsigned

    bleu Rsrc1, Src2, label

Conditionally branch to the instruction at the label if the contents of register Rsrc1 are less than or equal to Src2.

blez
Branch on less than equal zero

```
blez Rsrc, label
```

Conditionally branch to the instruction at the label if the contents of Rsrc are less than or equal to 0.

ble†
Branch on less than equal

```
ble Rsrc1, Src2, label
```

Conditionally branch to the instruction at the label if the contents of register Rsrc1 are less than or equal to Src2.

bltu†
Branch on less than unsigned

```
bltu Rsrc1, Src2, label
```

Conditionally branch to the instruction at the label if the contents of register Rsrc1 are less than Src2.

bltzal
Branch on less than and link

```
bltzal Rsrc, label
```

Conditionally branch to the instruction at the label if the contents of Rsrc are less than 0. Save the address of the next instruction in register 31.

bltz
Branch on less than zero

```
bltz Rsrc, label
```

Conditionally branch to the instruction at the label if the contents of Rsrc are less than 0.

blt†

Branch on less than

```
blt Rsrc1, Src2, label
```

Conditionally branch to the instruction at the label if the contents of register Rsrc1 are less than Src2.

bnez†

Branch on not equal zero

```
bnez Rsrc, label
```

Conditionally branch to the instruction at the label if the contents of Rsrc are not equal to 0.

bne

Branch on not equal

```
bne Rsrc1, Src2, label
```

Conditionally branch to the instruction at the label if the contents of register Rsrc1 are not equal to Src2.

break

Break

```
break n
```

Cause exception *n*. Exception 1 is reserved for the debugger.

b

Branch instruction

```
b label
```

Unconditionally branch to the instruction at the label.

c.eq.d

Compare equal double

```
c.eq.d FRsrc1, FRsrc2
```

Compare the floating point double in register FRsrc1 against the one in FRsrc2 and set the floating point condition flag true if they are equal.

c.eq.s

Compare equal single

```
c.eq.s FRsrc1, FRsrc2
```

Compare the floating point single in register FRsrc1 against the one in FRsrc2 and set the floating point condition flag true if they are equal.

c.le.d

Compare less than equal double

```
c.le.d FRsrc1, FRsrc2
```

Compare the floating point double in register FRsrc1 against the one in FRsrc2 and set the floating point condition flag true if the first is less than or equal to the second.

c.le.s

Compare less than equal single

```
c.le.s FRsrc1, FRsrc2
```

Compare the floating point single in register FRsrc1 against the one in FRsrc2 and set the floating point condition flag true if the first is less than or equal to the second.

c.lt.d

Compare less than double

```
c.lt.d FRsrc1, FRsrc2
```

Compare the floating point double in register FRsrc1 against the one in FRsrc2 and set the condition flag true if the first is less than the second.

c.lt.s

Comapre less than single

```
c.lt.s FRsrc1, FRsrc2
```

Compare the floating point single in register FRsrc1 against the one in FRsrc2 and set the condition flag true if the first is less than the second.

cvt.d.s   Convert single to double

```
cvt.d.s FRdest, FRsrc
```

Convert the single precision floating point number in register FRsrc to a double precision number and put it in register FRdest.

cvt.d.w   Convert integer to double

```
cvt.d.w FRdest, FRsrc
```

Convert the integer in register FRsrc to a double precision number and put it in register FRdest.

cvt.s.d   Convert double to single

```
cvt.s.d FRdest, FRsrc
```

Convert the double precision floating point number in register FRsrc to a single precision number and put it in register FRdest.

cvt.s.w   Convert integer to single

```
cvt.s.w. FRdest, FRsrc
```

Convert the integer in register FRsrc to a single number and put it in register FRdest.

cvt.w.d   Convert double to integer

```
cvt.w.d FRdest, FRsrc
```

Convert the double precision floating point number in register FRsrc to an integer and put it in register FRdest.

cvt.w.s   Convert single to integer

```
cvt.w.s FRdest, FRsrc
```

Convert the single precision floating point number in register FRsrc to an integer and put it in register FRdest.

div.d   Floating point divide double

```
div.d FRdest, FRsrc1, FRsrc2
```

Compute the quotient of the floating point doubles in registers FRsrc1 and FRsrc2 and put it in register FRdest.

div.s   Floating point divide single

```
div.s FRdest, FRsrc1, FRsrc2
```

Compute the quotient of the floating point singles in registers FRsrc1 and FRsrc3 and put it in register FRdest.

divu[†]   Divide (unsigned, without overflow)

```
divu Rdest, Rsrc1, Src2
```

Put the quotient of the integers from register Rsrc1 and Src2 into register Rdest. divu treats its operands as unsigned values.

divu   Divide (unsigned)

```
divu Rsrc1, Rsrc2
```

Divide the contents of the two registers. divu treats its operands as unsigned values. Leave the quotient in register lo and the remainder in register hi. Note that if an operand is negative, the remainder is unspecified by the MIPS architecture and depends on the conventions of the machine on which SPIM is run.

div†   Divide (signed, with overflow)

```
div Rdest, Rsrc1, Src2
```

Put the quotient of the integers from register `Rsrc1` and `Src2` into register `Rdest`.

div   Divide (signed)

```
div Rsrc1, Rsrc2
```

Divide the contents of the two registers. Leave the quotient in register `lo` and the remainder in register `hi`. Note that if an operand is negative, the remainder is unspecified by the MIPS architecture and depends on the conventions of the machine on which SPIM is run.

jalr   Jump and link register

```
jalr Rsrc
```

Unconditionally jump to the instruction whose address is in register `Rsrc`. Save the address of the next instruction in register 31.

jal   Jump and link

```
jal label
```

Unconditionally jump to the instruction at the label. Save the address of the next instruction in register 31.

jr   Jump register

```
jr Rsrc
```

Unconditionally jump to the instruction whose address is in register `Rsrc`.

j

Jump

```
j label
```

Unconditionally jump to the instruction at the label.

l.d†

Load floating point double

```
l.d FRdest, address
```

Load the floating point double at address into register FRdest.

l.s†

Load floating point single

```
l.s FRdest, address
```

Load the floating point single at address into register FRdest.

la†

Load address

```
la Rdest, address
```

Load computed *address*, not the contents of the location, into register Rdest.

lbu

Load unsigned byte

```
lbu Rdest, address
```

Load the byte at *address* into register Rdest. The byte is not sign-extended by the lbu instruction.

lb

Load byte

```
lb Rdest, address
```

Load the byte at *address* into register Rdest. The byte is sign-extended by the lb instruction.

ld†

Load double-word

```
ld Rdest, address
```

Load the 64-bit quantity at *address* into registers Rdest and Rdest + 1.

lhu

Load unsigned halfword

```
lhu Rdest, address
```

Load the 16-bit quantity (halfword) at *address* into register Rdest. The halfword is not sign-extended by the lhu instruction.

lh

Load halfword

```
lh Rdest, address
```

Load the 16-bit quantity (halfword) at *address* into register Rdest. The halfword is sign-extended by the lh instruction.

li†

Load immediate

```
li Rdest, imm
```

Move the immediate imm into register Rdest.

lui

Load upper immediate

```
lui Rdest, imm
```

Load the lower halfword of the immediate imm into the upper halfword of register Rdest. The lower bits of the register are set to 0.

lwc*z*

Load word coprocessor

```
lwcz Rdest, address
```

Load the word at *address* into register Rdest of coprocessor *z* (0–3).

lwl
Load word left

    lwl Rdest, address

Load the left bytes from the word at the possibly-unaligned *address* into register Rdest.

lwr
Load word right

    lwr Rdest, address

Load the right bytes from the word at the possibly-unaligned *address* into register Rdest.

lw
Load word

    lw Rdest, address

Load the 32-bit quantity (word) at *address* into register Rdest.

mfc1.d†
Move double from coprocessor 1

    mfc1.d Rdest, FRsrc1

Move the contents of floating point registers FRsrc1 and FRsrc1 + 1 to CPU registers Rdest and Rdest + 1.

mfc*z*
Move from coprocessor *z*

    mfcz Rdest, CPsrc

Move the contents of coprocessor *z*'s register CPsrc to CPU register Rdest.

mfhi
Move from hi

    mfhi Rdest

Move the contents of the hi register to register Rdest.

mflo

Move from lo

    mflo Rdest

Move the contents of the lo register to register Rdest.

mov.d

Move floating point double

    mov.d FRdest, FRsrc

Move the floating point double from register FRsrc to register FRdest.

mov.s

Move floating point single

    mov.s FRdest, FRsrc

Move the floating point single from register FRsrc to register FRdest.

move†

Move

    move Rdest, Rsrc

Move the contents of Rsrc to Rdest.

mtc*z*

Move to coprocessor *z*

    mtcz Rsrc, CPdest

Move the contents of CPU register Rsrc to coprocessor *z*'s register CPdest.

mthi

Move to hi

    mthi Rdest

Move the contents register Rdest to the hi register.

mtlo

Move to lo

```
mtlo Rdest
```

Move the contents register `Rdest` to the `lo` register.

mul.d

Floating point multiply double

```
mul.d FRdest, FRsrc1, FRsrc2
```

Compute the product of the floating point doubles in registers `Frsrc1` and `FRsrc2` and put it in register `FRdest`.

mul.s

Floating point multiply single

```
mul.s FRdest, FRsrc1, FRsrc2
```

Compute the product of the floating point singles in registers `FRsrc1` and `FRsrc2` and put it in register `FRdest`.

mulou†

Unsigned multiply (with overflow)

```
mulou Rdest, Rsrc1, Src2
```

Put the product of the integers from register `Rsrc1` and `Src2` into register `Rdest`.

mulo†

Multiply (with overflow)

```
mulo Rdest, Rsrc1, Src2
```

Put the product of the integers from register `Rsrc1` and `Src2` into register `Rdest`.

multu

Unsigned multiply

```
multu Rsrc1, Rsrc2
```

Multiply the contents of the two registers. Leave the low-order word of the product in register `lo` and the high-word in register `hi`.

mult

Multiply

        mult Rsrc1, Rsrc2

Multiply the contents of the two registers. Leave the low-order word of the product in register `lo` and the high-word in register `hi`.

mul[†]

Multiply (without overflow)

        mul Rdest, Rsrc1, Src2

Put the product of the integers from register `Rsrc1` and `Src2` into register `Rdest`.

neg.d

Negate double

        neg.d FRdest, FRsrc

Negate the floating point double in register `FRsrc` and put it in register `FRdest`.

neg.s

Negate single

        neg.s FRdest, FRsrc

Negate the floating point single in register `FRsrc` and put it in register `FRdest`.

negu[†]

Negate value (without overflow)

        negu Rdest, Rsrc

Put the negative of the integer from register `Rsrc` into register `Rdest`.

neg[†]

Negate value (with overflow)

        neg Rdest, Rsrc

Put the negative of the integer from register `Rsrc` into register `Rdest`.

nop   No operation

```
nop
```

Do nothing.

nor   NOR

```
nor Rdest, Rsrc1, Src2
```

Put the logical NOR of the integers from register Rsrc1 and Src2 into register Rdest.

not†   NOT

```
not Rdest, Rsrc
```

Put the bitwise logical negation of the integer from register Rsrc into register Rdest.

ori   OR immediate

```
ori Rdest, Rsrc1, Imm
```

Put the logical OR of the integers from register Rsrc1 and Imm into register Rdest.

or   OR

```
or Rdest, Rsrc1, Src2
```

Put the logical OR of the integers from register Rsrc1 and Src2 into register Rdest.

remu†   Unsigned remainder

```
remu Rdest, Rsrc1, Src2
```

Put the remainder from dividing the integer in register Rsrc1 by the integer in Src2 into register Rdest. Note that if an operand is negative, the remainder is unspecified by the MIPS architecture and depends on the conventions of the machine on which SPIM is run.

rem†

Remainder

        rem Rdest, Rsrc1, Src2

Put the remainder from dividing the integer in register `Rsrc1` by the integer in `Src2` into register `Rdest`. Note that if an operand is negative, the remainder is unspecified by the MIPS architecture and depends on the conventions of the machine on which SPIM is run.

rfe

Return from exception

        rfe

Restore the Status register.

rol†

Rotate left

        rol Rdest, Rsrc1, Src2

Rotate the contents of register `Rsrc1` left by the distance indicated by `Src2` and put the result in register `Rdest`.

ror†

Rotate right

        ror Rdest, Rsrc1, Src2

Rotate the contents of register `Rsrc1` right by the distance indicated by `Src2` and put the result in register `Rdest`.

s.d†

Store floating point double

        s.d FRdest, address

Store the floating point double in register `FRdest` at `address`.

s.s†

Store floating point single

```
s.s FRdest, address
```

Store the floating point single in register `FRdest` at `address`.

sb

Store byte

```
sb Rsrc, address
```

Store the low byte from register `Rsrc` at *address*.

sd†

Store double-word

```
sd Rsrc, address
```

Store the 64-bit quantity in registers `Rsrc` and `Rsrc + 1` at *address*.

seq†

Set equal

```
seq Rdest, Rsrc1, Src2
```

Set register `Rdest` to 1 if register `Rsrc1` equals `Src2` and to be 0 otherwise.

sgeu†

Set greater than equal unsigned

```
sgeu Rdest, Rsrc1, Src2
```

Set register `Rdest` to 1 if register `Rsrc1` is greater than or equal to `Src2` and to 0 otherwise.

sge†

Set greater than equal

```
sge Rdest, Rsrc1, Src2
```

Set register `Rdest` to 1 if register `Rsrc1` is greater than or equal to `Src2` and to 0 otherwise.

sgtu†

Set greater than unsigned

        sgtu Rdest, Rsrc1, Src2

Set register Rdest to 1 if register Rsrc1 is greater than Src2 and to 0 otherwise.

sgt†

Set greater than

        sgt Rdest, Rsrc1, Src2

Set register Rdest to 1 if register Rsrc1 is greater than Src2 and to 0 otherwise.

sh

Store halfword

        sh Rsrc, address

Store the low halfword from register Rsrc at *address*.

sleu†

Set less than equal unsigned

        sleu Rdest, Rsrc1, Src2

Set register Rdest to 1 if register Rsrc1 is less than or equal to Src2 and to 0 otherwise.

sle†

Set less than equal

        sle Rdest, Rsrc1, Src2

Set register Rdest to 1 if register Rsrc1 is less than or equal to Src2 and to 0 otherwise.

sllv
Shift left logical variable

        sllv Rdest, Rsrc1, Rsrc2

Shift the contents of register Rsrc1 left by the distance indicated by Rsrc2 and put the result in register Rdest.

sll
Shift left logical

        sll Rdest, Rsrc1, Src2

Shift the contents of register Rsrc1 left by the distance indicated by Src2 and put the result in register Rdest.

sltiu
Set less than unsigned immediate

        sltiu Rdest, Rsrc1, Imm

Set register Rdest to 1 if register Rsrc1 is less than Imm and to 0 otherwise.

slti
Set less than immediate

        slti Rdest, Rsrc1, Imm

Set register Rdest to 1 if register Rsrc1 is less than Imm and to 0 otherwise.

sltu
Set less than unsigned

        sltu Rdest, Rsrc1, Src2

Set register Rdest to 1 if register Rsrc1 is less than Src2 and to 0 otherwise.

slt
set less than

        slt Rdest, Rsrc1, Src2

Set register Rdest to 1 if register Rsrc1 is less than Src2 and to 0 otherwise.

sne[†]

Set not equal

```
sne Rdest, Rsrc1, Src2
```

Set register Rdest to 1 if register Rsrc1 is not equal to Src2 and to 0 otherwise.

srav

Shift right arithmetic variable

```
srav Rdest, Rsrc1, Rsrc2
```

Shift the contents of register Rsrc1 right by the distance indicated by Rsrc2 and put the result in register Rdest.

sra

Shift right arithmetic

```
sra Rdest, Rsrc1, Src2
```

Shift the contents of register Rsrc1 right by the distance indicated by Src2 and put the result in register Rdest.

srlv

Shift right logical variable

```
srlv Rdest, Rsrc1, Rsrc2
```

Shift the contents of register Rsrc1 right by the distance indicated by Rsrc2 and put the result in register Rdest.

srl

Shift right logical

```
srl Rdest, Rsrc1, Src2
```

Shift the contents of register Rsrc1 right by the distance indicated by Src2 and put the result in register Rdest.

sub.d
Floating point subtract double

```
sub.d FRdest, FRsrc1, FRsrc2
```

Compute the difference of the floating point doubles in registers FRsrc1 and FRsrc2 and put it in register FRdest.

sub.s
Floating point subtract single

```
sub.s FRdest, FRsrc1, FRsrc2
```

Compute the difference of the floating point singles in registers FRsrc1 and FRsrc2 and put it in register FRdest.

subu
Subtract (without overflow)

```
subu Rdest, Rsrc1, Src2
```

Put the difference of the integers from register Rsrc1 and Src2 into register Rdest.

sub
Subtract (with overflow)

```
sub Rdest, Rsrc1, Src2
```

Put the difference of the integers from register Rsrc1 and Src2 into register Rdest.

swc$z$
Store word coprocessor

```
swcz Rsrc, address
```

Store the word from register Rsrc of coprocessor z at *address*.

swl
Store word left

```
swl Rsrc, address
```

Store the left bytes from register Rsrc at the possibly unaligned *address*.

swr
Store word right

```
swr Rsrc, address
```

Store the right bytes from register `Rsrc` at the possibly unaligned *address*.

sw
Store word

```
sw Rsrc, address
```

Store the word from register `Rsrc` at *address*.

syscall
System call

```
syscall
```

Register $v0 contains the number of the system call provided by SPIM.

ulhu[†]
Unaligned load halfword unsigned

```
ulhu Rdest, address
```

Load the 16-bit quantity (halfword) at the possibly unaligned *address* into register `Rdest`. The halfword is not sign-extended by the `ulhu` instruction.

ulh[†]
Unaligned load halfword

```
ulh Rdest, address
```

Load the 16-bit quantity (halfword) at the possibly unaligned *address* into register `Rdest`. The halfword is sign-extended by the `ulh` instruction.

ulw[†]
Unaligned load word

```
ulw Rdest, address
```

Load the 32-bit quantity (word) at the possibly unaligned *address* into register `Rdest`.

ush†

Unaligned store halfword

```
ush Rsrc, address
```

Store the low halfword from register `Rsrc` at the possibly unaligned *address*.

usw†

Unaligned store word

```
usw Rsrc, address
```

Store the word from register `Rsrc` at the possibly unaligned *address*.

xori

XOR immediate

```
xori Rdest, Rsrc1, Imm
```

Put the logical XOR of the integers from register `Rsrc1` and `Imm` into register `Rdest`.

xor

XOR

```
xor Rdest, Rsrc1, Src2
```

Put the logical XOR of the integers from register `Rsrc1` and `Src2` into register `Rdest`.

Index